Current Controversies

Media Trustworthiness

Other Books in the Current Controversies Series

America's Role in a Changing World
Artificial Intelligence and the Future of Humanity
Big Tech and Democracy
The Business of College Sports: Who Earns What
The Capitol Riot: Fragile Democracy
Climate Change and Biodiversity
Cyberterrorism
Domestic Extremism
The Politics and Science of COVID-19
Reparations for Black Americans
Space: Tourism, Competition, Militarization

Current Controversies

Media Trustworthiness

Kathryn Roberts, Book Editor

GREENHAVEN PUBLISHING

Published in 2023 by Greenhaven Publishing, LLC
29 E. 21st Street
New York, NY 10010

First Edition

Articles in Greenhaven Publishing anthologies are often edited for length to meet page requirements. In addition, original titles of these works are changed to clearly present the main thesis and to explicitly indicate the author's opinion. Every effort is made to ensure that Greenhaven Publishing accurately reflects the original intent of the authors. Every effort has been made to trace the owners of the copyrighted material.

Cover image: metamorworks/Shutterstock.com

Library of Congress Cataloging-in-Publication Data

Names: Roberts, Kathryn, 1990– editor.
Title: Media trustworthiness / Kathryn Roberts, book editor.
Description: First edition. | New York : Greenhaven Publishing, 2023. | Series: Current controversies | Includes bibliographical references and index. | Audience: Ages 15+ | Audience: Grades 10–12 | Summary: "Anthology of essays exploring the decline in Americans' trust in media"— Provided by publisher.
Identifiers: LCCN 2022003858 | ISBN 9781534508989 (library binding) | ISBN 9781534508972 (paperback) | ISBN 9781534508996 (ebook)
Subjects: LCSH: Journalistic ethics—United States. | Mass media—Moral and ethical aspects—United States. | Journalism—Social aspects—United States. | Mass media—Social aspects—United States.
Classification: LCC PN4888.E8 M423 2023 | DDC 174/.90713—dc23/eng/20220215
LC record available at https://lccn.loc.gov/2022003858

Manufactured in the United States of America

Website: http://greenhavenpublishing.com

Contents

Foreword

"Controversy" is a word that has an undeniably unpleasant connotation. It carries a definite negative charge. Controversy can spoil family gatherings, spread a chill around classroom and campus discussion, inflame public discourse, open raw civic wounds, and lead to the ouster of public officials. We often feel that controversy is almost akin to bad manners, a rude and shocking eruption of that which must not be spoken or thought of in polite, tightly guarded society. To avoid controversy, to quell controversy, is often seen as a public good, a victory for etiquette, perhaps even a moral or ethical imperative.

Yet the studious, deliberate avoidance of controversy is also a whitewashing, a denial, a death threat to democracy. It is a false sterilizing and sanitizing and superficial ordering of the messy, ragged, chaotic, at times ugly processes by which a healthy democracy identifies and confronts challenges, engages in passionate debate about appropriate approaches and solutions, and arrives at something like a consensus and a broadly accepted and supported way forward. Controversy is the megaphone, the speaker's corner, the public square through which the citizenry finds and uses its voice. Controversy is the life's blood of our democracy and absolutely essential to the vibrant health of our society.

Our present age is certainly no stranger to controversy. We are consumed by fierce debates about technology, privacy, political correctness, poverty, violence, crime and policing, guns, immigration, civil and human rights, terrorism, militarism, environmental protection, and gender and racial equality. Loudly competing voices are raised every day, shouting opposing opinions, putting forth competing agendas, and summoning starkly different visions of a utopian or dystopian future. Often these voices attempt to shout the others down; there is precious little listening and considering among the cacophonous din. Yet listening and considering, too, are essential to the health of a democracy. If controversy is democracy's lusty lifeblood, respectful listening and careful thought are its higher faculties, its brain, its conscience.

Current Controversies does not shy away from or attempt to hush the loudly competing voices. It seeks to provide readers with as wide and representative as possible a range of articulate voices on any given controversy of the day, separates each one out to allow it to be heard clearly and fairly, and encourages careful listening to each of these well-crafted, thoughtfully expressed opinions, supplied by some of today's leading academics, thinkers, analysts, politicians, policy makers, economists, activists, change agents, and advocates. Only after listening to a wide range of opinions on an issue, evaluating the strengths and weaknesses of each argument, assessing how well the facts and available evidence mesh with the stated opinions and conclusions, and thoughtfully and critically examining one's own beliefs and conscience can the reader begin to arrive at his or her own conclusions and articulate his or her own stance on the spotlighted controversy.

This process is facilitated and supported in each Current Controversies volume by an introduction and chapter overviews that provide readers with the essential context they need to begin engaging with the spotlighted controversies, with the debates surrounding them, and with their own perhaps shifting or nascent opinions on them. Chapters are organized around several key questions that are answered with diverse opinions representing all points on the political spectrum. In its content, organization, and methodology, readers are encouraged to determine the authors' point of view and purpose, interrogate and analyze the various arguments and their rhetoric and structure, evaluate the arguments' strengths and weaknesses, test their claims against available facts and evidence, judge the validity of the reasoning, and bring into clearer, sharper focus the reader's own beliefs and conclusions and how they may differ from or align with those in the collection or those of classmates.

Research has shown that reading comprehension skills improve dramatically when students are provided with compelling, intriguing, and relevant "discussable" texts. The subject matter of these collections could not be more compelling, intriguing, or urgently relevant to today's students and the world they are poised to inherit. The anthologized articles also provide the basis for stimulating, lively, and passionate classroom debates. Students who are compelled to anticipate objections to their own argument and identify the flaws in those of an opponent read more carefully, think more critically, and steep themselves in relevant context, facts, and information more thoroughly. In short, using discussable text of the kind provided by every single volume in the Current Controversies series encourages close reading, facilitates reading comprehension, fosters research, strengthens critical thinking, and greatly enlivens and energizes classroom discussion and participation. The entire learning process is deepened, extended, and strengthened.

If we are to foster a knowledgeable, responsible, active, and engaged citizenry, we must provide readers with the intellectual, interpretive, and critical-thinking tools and experience necessary to make sense of the world around them and of the all-important debates and arguments that inform it. We must encourage them not to run away from or attempt to quell controversy but to embrace it in a responsible, conscientious, and thoughtful way, to sharpen and strengthen their own informed opinions by listening to and critically analyzing those of others. This series encourages respectful engagement with and analysis of current controversies and competing opinions and fosters a resulting increase in the strength and rigor of one's own opinions and stances. As such, it helps readers assume their rightful place in the public square and provides them with the skills necessary to uphold their awesome responsibility—guaranteeing the continued and future health of a vital, vibrant, and free democracy.

Introduction

> *"Consumers are their own editors and program executives, selecting content that fits their tastes, ideology, and political leaning. They vote with their mouse and clicker, selecting content they want when they want it. And they have countless options satisfying their partisan preferences."*
>
> —*Tobe Berkovitz, Boston University*

According to Gallup, an American analytics and advisory company, in 2021, trust in the traditional media was at an all-time low. Even worse, the United States ranked dead last in a 2021 survey by Reuters of 46 countries on media trust.

But it hasn't always been this way. Although there has always existed an undercurrent of skepticism of the news and media in society, even when the news media is seen at its most favorable, in recent years in the United States that mistrust has eroded significantly, starting in 1987 when the US Federal Communications Commission (FCC) abolished the Fairness Doctrine.

Introduced in 1949, the Fairness Doctrine was a policy that required the holders of broadcast licenses both to present controversial issues of public importance and to do so in a manner that fairly reflected differing viewpoints. The Fairness Doctrine was revoked after a campaign that asserted it was an infringement of free speech and intruded on broadcasters' journalistic judgment.

This shift allowed news organizations to brand themselves as "unfiltered." The first notable instance was in 1988, when Rush Limbaugh received a national broadcast contract that allowed him to share content that trafficked in conspiracy theories, divisiveness, and even viciousness, all content that would have been removed from the airwaves under the Fairness Doctrine.

But it is not just the revocation of the Fairness Doctrine—which could be reinstated at any time by the FCC, with enough public pressure—that has led society to this point where only 36 percent of people have either "a great deal" or "a fair amount" of trust and confidence in newspapers, television, and radio news reporting. Whether it's the unchecked proliferation of fake news on social media giants like Facebook and Twitter, major political figures making unfounded claims that the media is not to be trusted, or increased political divisiveness, people today look for news that fits their own personal biases and refuse to be swayed by anything offering a differing perspective.

It was only in late 2020 and early 2021 that social media platforms like Facebook and Twitter started taking a stand on accounts that consistently shared false or misleading information, like former president Donald Trump's Twitter account. But given the extremely divisive 2020 presidential election, the January 6th insurrection at the US Capitol, and the COVID-19 pandemic, are those actions too little, too late?

Additionally, is it possible to undo the damage done by intentional erosion of public trust in the media by people like former president Trump, who would openly and incorrectly claim that fact-based news reports were fake news?

Fake news is defined as false or misleading information presented as news and as facts by the media. According to Merriam-Webster, the term was first used in the 1890s, in reports from the *Cincinnati Commercial Tribune* (Cincinnati, OH), the *Kearney Daily Hub* (Kearney, NE), and the *Buffalo Commercial* (Buffalo, NY). And while the concept of fake news was co-opted in 2016 during Trump's first presidential campaign, one of the most recent times in history that the term was used was in Nazi Germany. The Nazis used the term *Lügenpresse*, telling citizens that organizations that did not report favorably on the Nazi Party were the "lying press," which led to a significant erosion of public trust so severe that use of the term is extremely unpopular in Germany today.

With the current state of affairs in the United States and around the world, is it possible to restore public trust in the media? A democracy cannot function properly without a strong, trustworthy media, but what does it mean to report facts? Until society can first determine what "fake news" means, it will be extremely challenging to make meaningful strides toward that restoration of trust.

While transparency is one of the many critical factors, current and emerging technologies must be equipped to properly identify and control the spread of fake news and misinformation in the online space. But as private entities, there is a question of how to properly, appropriately, and legally manage how tech platforms like Facebook and Twitter and future organizations like them manage false and misleading information.

The diverse viewpoints contained in *Current Controversies: Media Trustworthiness* delve into the complicated world of fake news, media bias, and eroded public trust, exploring why people do or do not trust the media and what can be done to create a future with more credible news reporting.

Chapter 1

Is the Traditional News Media Trustworthy?

Overview: What Makes the News Trustworthy?

John Gramlich

John Gramlich is a senior writer/editor at the Pew Research Center, where he writes about criminal justice and immigration. The Pew Research Center is a nonpartisan, non-advocacy "fact tank" that carries out surveys and other social science research to learn about the issues, attitudes, and trends shaping the US and the world.

Americans see a variety of factors as important when it comes to deciding whether a news story is trustworthy or not, but their attitudes vary by party affiliation, demographic characteristics and news consumption habits, according to a recent Pew Research Center survey.

Overall, broad majorities of U.S. adults say it is at least somewhat important to consider each of five surveyed factors when determining whether a news story is trustworthy or not: the news organization that publishes it (88%); the sources cited in it (86%); their gut instinct about it (77%); the person, if any, who shared it with them (68%); and the specific journalist who reported it (66%). Just 24% of adults say it's at least somewhat important to consider a sixth factor included in the survey: whether the story has a lot of shares, comments or likes on social media.

But notably fewer Americans see each of these factors as very important. Half of U.S. adults point to the news organization that publishes a story as a very important factor when determining its trustworthiness, while a similar share (47%) point to the sources that are cited in it. Fewer cite their gut instinct about the story (30%), the specific journalist who reported it (24%), the person who shared it with them (23%) or the engagement it has received

"What Makes a News Story Trustworthy? Americans Point to the Outlet That Publishes It, Sources Cited," by John Gramlich, Pew Research Center, June 9, 2021. Reprinted by permission.

on social media (6%), according to the March 8-14 survey of 12,045 adults. The survey was part of a broader study of media coverage of President Joe Biden's first 60 days in office.

Democrats and Democratic-leaning independents are slightly more likely than Republicans and GOP leaners to say it's very important to consider the news organization that publishes a story (55% vs. 47%) and the sources that are cited in it (51% vs. 44%). Republicans, in turn, are more likely than Democrats to see their own gut instinct as very important (35% vs. 26%), though this is a minority view in both parties.

Older Americans are generally more likely than younger Americans to point to the news organization that publishes a story and the sources that are cited in it as critical factors when determining its trustworthiness. For example, among those 65 and older, 57% say the news organization is a very important factor and 54% say the same about the sources cited. Smaller proportions of adults under 30 see these as very important factors (42% and 41%, respectively). These findings are consistent with previous Pew Research Center studies, which found that younger Americans tend to feel less connected to their sources of news and are less likely to remember the sources of online news links they clicked on.

When it comes to education, 59% of adults with a college degree say it's very important to consider the news organization that publishes a story, and 54% say the same of the sources that are cited in it. That compares with around four-in-ten of those with a high school diploma or less education (43% and 40%, respectively). Conversely, those with a high school diploma or less are more likely than those with a college degree to see the other factors asked about as very important when determining a news story's trustworthiness.

Black Americans are more likely than those in other racial and ethnic groups to see some factors as very important when determining the trustworthiness of a news story. For example, around four-in-ten Black adults (38%) point to their own gut instinct as a very important factor, compared with three-in-ten or fewer White (30%), Hispanic (26%) and Asian American adults (22%).

Black adults are also more likely than other Americans to point to the specific journalist who reported the story and the person who shared it with them; about a third of Black adults say these are very important factors to consider.

Avid news followers are more likely to see all of the factors asked about in the survey as critical when deciding on a news story's trustworthiness. For instance, Americans who are very closely following news about the Biden administration are especially likely to say it's very important to consider the news organization that publishes a story (69%) and the sources that are cited in it (65%). Among those who are following Biden administration news less closely, fewer see these factors as very important.

Most Americans Pay Attention to the Sources Cited in News Stories

In addition to asking about the factors that the public considers when deciding whether a news story is trustworthy, the survey asked Americans how closely they pay attention to the sources they see in the news. Overall, 22% of U.S. adults say they pay very close attention to the sources that are cited in news stories, while another 45% say they pay somewhat close attention.

Democrats are slightly more likely than Republicans to say they pay very close attention to the sources cited in news stories (25% vs. 19%)—a finding that aligns with the fact that Democrats are more likely than Republicans to see sourcing as very important to a story's trustworthiness. Americans ages 65 and older (27%), those with a college degree (27%) and Black adults (28%) are also especially likely to say they pay very close attention to the sources that are mentioned in news stories.

Americans who have been following news about the Biden administration very closely are again the most likely to say they pay very close attention to the sources cited in news stories. Nearly half of these Americans (47%) say this, compared with smaller shares of those who follow news about the Biden administration fairly closely (20%) or not too or not at all closely (8%).

News Organizations Can Increase the Public's Trust

Lisa Heyamoto and Todd Milbourn

Lisa Heyamoto is a narrative journalist and journalism educator whose research, teaching, and creative work focuses on community-building through storytelling. Todd Milbourn is an investigative reporter and journalism instructor who co-founded the 32 Percent Project, a national community engagement project exploring what drives and disrupts trust in the news media.

In August, nearly 400 news outlets made the case for the importance of journalism in response to President Donald Trump's repeated claim that the media is "the enemy of the people."

In #FreePress editorials published in newspapers across the country, writers stressed journalism's role in a democracy, and that a free press is essential to a free society.

The message came at a time when anti-press rhetoric is soaring and concerns about inaccuracy and bias in the news have meant Americans' trust in the media is lingering near all-time lows.

Yet our research suggests that if news organizations are truly going to close the trust gap, they must go beyond explanations of what journalism means to democracy and directly make the case for what it means to citizens.

As researchers and journalists, we launched The 32 Percent Project to explore how citizens define trust and how news organizations can better earn it. Named for the percentage of Americans who had confidence in the news media in 2016, the project was guided by the principle that the best way to discover what citizens want is to ask them.

We held public conversations with 54 people in four communities across the country, asking questions about what news organizations should do to increase public trust. Here are four insights from those conversations:

1. Open Up the Black Box

How do reporters decide what goes into a news story? Where is the line between fact and opinion? Are the advertisers who fund the news determining what reporters cover?

To many journalists, the answers to these questions may seem self-evident. To many non-journalists, they are a mystery. Many workshop participants reported that they have little knowledge of how news is produced, which makes them skeptical of what they read, hear and see.

If news organizations are going to earn their trust, citizens said they must take active steps to communicate both their mission and their methods. Participants said this could mean anything from making unedited interviews available to explaining journalistic terms to opening newsrooms for public tours.

When it comes to restoring trust between citizens and the press, a community college student in California said journalists need to prioritize authentic, clear communication.

"You don't want people to talk at you," the student said. "You want people to talk with you."

2. Create a Shared Mission

Many journalists view themselves as independent watchdogs of powerful institutions, which means they may produce articles critical of those institutions and their leaders. And while conversation participants reported that they value the watchdog function, many said news organizations must first establish their role as a good neighbor.

Citizens wanted to know that a news outlet explicitly shares the community's values and that everyone is working together toward a shared goal. To some, that meant doing journalism as a member of a community rather than as an outside observer. To others, it meant demanding that news organizations place their public service mission ahead of short-term profits.

Journalists, they said, must approach their work as a more direct service to community members, and devote time, money and energy to building deep, reciprocal relationships with their readers, viewers and listeners.

Without a sense of common mission, many participants said they'd continue to see news organizations as working for advertisers—not for them.

3. No Diversity, No Trust

Across all conversations, participants said they did not see themselves or their lives reflected in the news they consume. They said journalists understandably produce stories that arise from their personal backgrounds and experiences, but noted that people of color and those who live in rural areas, for example, are not well represented in media organizations. Homogeneous newsrooms, they said, tend to produce homogeneous stories.

This conveys to those groups that the news isn't for them, participants said, while depriving all news consumers of a richer picture of American life.

"It's one of the reasons why rural and small-town people are trusting the media less and less," said a participant in rural Illinois. "When they see the coverage of their own setting, either the interpretation is off or they're really missing some important piece of the story."

Diversity, we found, is fundamental to earning trust. If newsrooms want to gain credibility, they must broadly and authentically mirror the makeup of their audience.

4. Emphasize the Positive

One of the most common complaints we heard was that the news is too negative. And though stories about crime, car crashes and corruption may earn an audience's attention, they don't appear to do much to earn long-term trust.

"When there is something good going in my neighborhood, I don't see it," said a community activist in Boston. "But if somebody shoots somebody, oh, first page."

Research participants said they want the news to more closely reflect the general positive sense they experience in their day-to-day lives. But that doesn't mean they're interested solely in feel-good coverage. Rather, many participants pointed to a need for more stories that focus on solutions to problems rather than just the problems.

Takeaways

If news organizations want to earn public trust, a compelling place to start would be to mirror the characteristics of trusted interpersonal relationships. That means being consistent, transparent, authentic, positive and conveying a respect for diversity alongside a sense of shared mission.

"Journalism is a relationship," said a participant in suburban Los Angeles. "It's not a product."

One of the #FreePress editorials to best capture that spirit came from the *San Diego Union-Tribune*. The author took the opportunity to highlight the paper's recently launched "Our Journalism, Explained" section, which engages readers in a conversation about the paper's journalistic standards and practices.

As the editorial suggests and our research confirmed, trust isn't something news organizations can simply ask for—it's something they must repeatedly earn.

The 24/7 News Cycle Promotes Anxiety and Stress

Eric Patterson, MSCP

Eric Patterson, MSCP, NCC, LPC, is a professional counselor who has been working for over a decade to help children, adolescents, and adults reach their goals and improve their well-being. Along the way, he worked as a collaborating investigator for the field trials of the DSM-5 and completed an agreement to provide mental health treatment to underserved communities with the National Health Service Corp.

Whether it's the coronavirus (COVID-19), political divisiveness, threats of terrorism, or mass shootings in malls, churches, and schools, it seems like there is always something to worry about. You might not be immediately affected by these issues, but the constant exposure to 24-hour news and social media, which is often heavily skewed toward the negative, can adversely influence your mental health and overall well-being.

If you're finding yourself becoming more and more anxious in the face of a constant barrage of bad news, you're not alone. Here you'll find ways to disconnect from a relentlessly distressing news cycle, engage in healthier outlets, and otherwise better protect yourself from this 21st century problem.

The Link Between News and Stress

There's no arguing the value of the news. Reporters and journalists work tirelessly to keep us informed. However, having access to too much information too often can be detrimental to certain aspects of your mental health and well-being.

As 24-hour news outlets compete for viewers, they often cover events in extreme detail or may even sensationalize aspects of the

"Dealing with Anxiety and Stress in the Age of the 24/7 News Cycle," by Eric Patterson, MSCP, American Addiction Centers, August 10, 2021. Reprinted by permission.

story to make the coverage more appealing. More than 70% of Americans believe the media "blows things out of proportion," which may seem harmless, but it could lead to increased stress and anxiety in the people who frequently consume this information.[1]

More than half of Americans say the news causes them stress.[1] In small doses, stress is not always problematic, but chronic stress is associated with numerous health issues (both physical and mental).[2] When it's so common to check and recheck for coverage accessible from multiple platforms such as your phone, your TV, and your car radio, you may find it impossible to escape both the news and the stress that comes with it. According to the American Psychological Association (APA), American adults report feeling conflicted between wanting to be informed but also feeling that the news contributes to their stress levels.[1]

Psychological Effects of 24/7 Bad News

While there are certainly feel-good stories out there, a large part of what is covered in the news is anything but positive or uplifting. Startling and unnerving headlines get views and clicks, and so the news tends to get saturated by stories that upset the reader. Today's news is also influenced by user-generated content (UGC). This includes images and videos that may depict graphic violence or other disturbing content that in the past would likely have been deemed too shocking or inappropriate for the public and consequently withheld.[3] Today, this type of content is sought-after by the news media and all-too-easy to see online, even by those who don't specifically seek it out.

Even when the coverage isn't especially graphic or disturbing, the consistent flow of anxiety-inducing topics can have a significant impact. We have access to more information than ever before, but all that information reportedly has a majority of Americans feeling the stress. In fact, more than 60% of Americans find the country's future to be a significant source of stress or strain for them, and almost as many (close to 60%) believe this to be the lowest point in U.S. history.

Arthur Evans, the CEO of the APA states: "With 24-hour news networks and conversations with friends, family and other connections on social media, it's hard to avoid the constant stream of stress around issues of national concern."[1]

Anxiety and Depression

Frequent exposure to troubling news can wear you down mentally. Before the advent of the 24-hour news cycle, the average person would typically read the paper in the morning or watch the evening news broadcast for their daily fill of national or global updates. But now the news comes at us from all angles, and in some cases it may cause psychological harm.

For example, many Americans find the news to be a source of stress,[1] and chronic stress is a risk factor for depression.[2] Non-stop exposure to this source of stress may lead a person to become depressed.

Anxiety is another concern for Americans who are inundated with news media. Constantly watching coverage of frightening events may lead you to worry that these events will happen to you. For example, a 10-year-old girl in Delhi who experienced a slight tremor from a far-away earthquake in Afghanistan developed anxiety symptoms after watching news coverage of the devastation and loss of life. She began fearing the same would happen to her and had to be treated with therapy and medication.[4]

One study of Israelis at the start of a war in Gaza found that those who increased their normal viewing of TV news were 1.6x more likely to develop anxiety symptoms than those who continued watching at their normal frequency.[5]

Not everyone who watches or reads a great deal of news will develop a mental health disorder, of course, but many people will experience some level of distress in relation to their news consumption. In 2016, a therapist coined the term "headline stress disorder" to describe the tension, worry, fear and sadness that arise from endless, negative news articles.[6]

Relationship Between Stress and Addiction

Stress, anxiety and depression are all associated with a risk of substance abuse.[7] Being notified of what's going wrong all throughout the day every day can motivate some people to reach for a drink or a drug to eases their worries or try to just forget about it all.

Using drugs or alcohol to cope with life's stressors is risky. Over time, problematic substance use of any kind could lead to the development of a substance use disorder (addiction). For recovering individuals, chronic stress may lead to relapse. In the face of unrelenting news coverage that gives you more to worry about, it's critical to moderate your media consumption and find healthy outlets to release stress.

How to Cope with Anxiety Caused by the Media

To break away from the cycle of breaking news:[6]

- Set time limits. How long are you consuming news each day—one hour, two hours, 10 hours? You may not even realize how much time you're dedicating to it if you regularly open news articles on your phone or tablet or view it on social media sites. To avoid overdoing it, set aside specific times of day, such as during your morning cup of coffee, to read or watch the news.
- Set source limits. With countless sources for news content online and on TV, information and opinions will vary, which may contribute to increased anxiety and doubt. Stick to two or three trusted sources of information and resist the urge to search for more from unreliable sites.
- Beware of social media. For all of its good, social media allows people to spread baseless claims freely. Unfollow untrustworthy news sites and consider blocking or simply unfollowing people whose posts lead to more anxiety and sadness.

Apart from setting limits on your news consumption, you can take proactive steps to reduce your stress so that you don't end up heading to the bar or using other drugs to feel better. To counteract stress, anxiety, and depression, try:[8, 9]

- Making and keeping meaningful connections. Friends and family provide much-needed support when you're feeling down or anxious. Make attempts to connect in person instead of relying on social media. Online, your connections may feel less substantive or meaningful and you'll continue to be at risk of exposing yourself to more news as well as the contentious comments attached to it. You may even be tempted to get involved in the arguments, which can cause more bad feelings.
- Volunteering your time. So much of news-related stress makes people feel like helpless observers of the situation, but when a person decides to volunteer their energy, they make a positive difference in the world. Not only does volunteering produce good feelings, it gives you an opportunity to make new friends who can serve as a source of emotional support.
- Seeking out the good news. The good news is always present, even if it is buried under countless reports of violence, hate, and greed. Make it your daily mission to find happy and uplifting stories as a reminder that good is out there.
- Staying physically healthy. Eating well, exercising, and getting restful sleep aid in the battle against stress. Taking time to unplug, prepare a meal, exercise, and turn in to bed early will fight back against news-related stress.
- Engaging in therapy. A therapist can help you work through your anxiety. If you're unable to make it to a therapy session, there are other options. Therapy apps and teletherapy are becoming increasingly available and can do a world of good when you can't see someone in person.

References

1. American Psychological Association. (2017). *APA Stress in America Survey: US at "Lowest Point We Can Remember;" Future of Nation Most Commonly Reported Source of Stress.*

2. Centre for Studies on Human Stress. (n.d.). *Acute vs. Chronic Stress.*

3. Feinstein, A., Audet, B., & Waknine, E. (2014). Witnessing Images of Extreme Violence: A Psychological Study of Journalists in the Newsroom, *JRSM Open.*

4. Bhatia, M. S., & Gautam, P. (2016). Case report of a child's anxiety disorder precipitated by tremors from a distant earthquake that was extensively covered in local news stories. *Shanghai archives of psychiatry*, 28(1), 52–55. https://doi .org/10.3969/j.issn.1002-0829.215112

5. Bodas, M., Siman-Toy, M., and Solomon, Z. (2015). Anxiety-Inducing Media: The Effect of Constant News Broadcasting on the Well-Being of Israeli Television Viewers, *Psychiatry*, 78(3).

6. Spector, Nicole. (2017). "Headline Stress Disorder": How to Cope with the Anxiety Caused by the 24/7 News Cycle, NBC News.

7. U.S. Department of Health & Human Services. (2019). *Mental Health and Substance Use Disorders.*

8. National Institute of Mental Health. (n.d.). *5 Things You Should Know About Stress.*

9. U.S. Department of Health & Human Services, Office on Women's Health. (2017). *Stress and your health.*

The US Media Is the Least Trustworthy in the World

Joe Concha

Joe Concha is an American media personality and political columnist working as a media and political columnist at The Hill *and as a contributor for Fox News Channel. He previously appeared on CNN and has been a columnist for Mediate, FoxSports.com, NBCSports .com, and the* New York Times.

The U.S. media is the least trustworthy in the world, according to a comprehensive new Reuters Institute survey encompassing 46 countries.

Yes, you read that right. The country with among the most resources in this arena—human, technical and otherwise—finished dead last. Finland ranked the highest, with a 65 percent trust rating. In Kenya, the trust rating clocked in at 61 percent.

But here in the U.S.A., the home of global media giants including the *New York Times*, *Washington Post* and CNN, we're trusted by a whopping 29 percent of those reading and watching.

Is anyone really surprised? Because in looking at polls over the past few years (even pre-Donald Trump) we've been trending in this dubious direction for some time.

For example, one Axios/Survey Monkey poll in 2019 found that nearly 8-in-10 independent voters said they believed that news organizations report news "they know to be fake, false or purposely misleading." Ninety-two percent of Republicans felt the same way, as did even a majority of Democrats.

Which means readers and viewers believe that the "mistakes" we so often see, particularly in the political media that dominates the national landscape, are not happening because of human error, which is a convenient excuse offered up from left-leaning

"US Just Finished Dead Last Among 46 Countries in Media Trust—Here's Why," by Joe Concha, The Hill, June 28, 2021. Reprinted by permission.

"journalists" when "bombshell" reports end up being false, fake or purposely misleading.

Russian collusion with the Trump campaign? The Mueller Report didn't find proof of that despite all the "evidence" Rep. Adam Schiff (D-Calif.) claimed he had but never produced. That "story" dominated the first three years of the Trump era regardless, so that two-thirds of Democratic voters believe the Russians actually altered vote tallies to tip the election from Hillary Clinton to Trump.

How about the bombshell Russian bounties of U.S. troops? Never happened.

How about that COVID-19 came from a Wuhan lab that studies coronaviruses and engages in gain-of-function research? We've gone from reckless conspiracy theory to somebody like Jon Stewart appearing on *The Late Show with Steven Colbert* to make the argument that it's a very real possibility.

I could go on and on but have finite space here. For dozens of more examples, check out Sharyl Attkisson's comprehensive list of media malfeasance over the past few years. She's currently up to 156 examples.

But it wasn't always this way. Back in 1976, in the days of anchors such as Walter Cronkite, John Chancellor, David Brinkley and Roger Mudd, nearly three-quarters of the country trusted the media, according to Gallup.

Fast forward to 2021, and the likes of Chris Cuomo, Jim Acosta, Brian Williams and Yamiche Alcindor are given the same prestigious titles of anchor or correspondent.

These aren't anchors, of course, they're patently partisan opinion hosts. All share their feelings, their opinions—which always support the blue team—and pass it off as objective news reporting. Which, of course, is an insult to those who have eyes and ears and brains.

And trust is like toothpaste: Once it's out of the tube, it's impossible to regain. Example: the *New York Times* hasn't endorsed a Republican presidential candidate in 65 years, which means the so-called paper of record endorsed Walter Mondale in 1984 and Michael Dukakis in 1988, who lost a combined 89 states.

Talk about being out of touch. The *Washington Post* has never endorsed a Republican presidential candidate in its history. CNN—once a beacon of solid, objective reporting in the Bernard Shaw/Gulf Wars era—has become a parody of itself in losing nearly 75 percent of its audience since the beginning of the year, an unprecedented drop.

In other words, don't expect the new Cronkites and Brinkleys of the world to swoop in and save journalism in the U.S. anytime soon.

Fortunately, the news we get on the local level has remained largely unchanged. Viewers get the big stories regarding crime, human interest, sports and the weather. Trust in local news hasn't changed much since 1976. The reason? Local news almost always keeps opinion out of its reporting, while national political media injects plenty of it, invariably in support of Democratic efforts, into stories outside of op-ed sections and in actual news stories.

One of the best studies on the move to opinion came in a 2019 RAND Corporation report that analyzed content from 15 print and television outlets over nearly three decades (1989 to 2017).

The newspapers studied were the *New York Times*, *Washington Post* and *St. Louis Post-Dispatch*, while CBS, NBC, ABC, CNN, Fox and MSNBC were analyzed on the TV front. Digital journalism was represented by Politico, the Blaze, Breitbart News, BuzzFeed Politics, the Daily Caller and the Huffington Post.

"The findings point to a gradual and subtle shift over time and between old and new media toward a more subjective form of journalism that is grounded in personal perspective," reads RAND's conclusion.

Not exactly facts first, but feelings first.

The U.S. is the least-trusted country of 46 when it comes to the way consumers view the news. If that isn't a wake-up call for the industry, I'm not sure what would be.

We Need to Reinstate the Fairness Doctrine

Steve Rendall

Steve Rendall is a senior analyst for the media watchdog organization Fairness and Accuracy in Reporting (FAIR), which was founded in 1986 by Jeff Cohen. Rendall is also co-host of FAIR's syndicated radio show CounterSpin, *which is heard on more than 125 noncommercial stations across the US and Canada.*

A license permits broadcasting, but the licensee has no constitutional right to be the one who holds the license or to monopolize a…frequency to the exclusion of his fellow citizens. There is nothing in the First Amendment which prevents the Government from requiring a licensee to share his frequency with others…. It is the right of the viewers and listeners, not the right of the broadcasters, which is paramount." (U.S. Supreme Court, upholding the constitutionality of the Fairness Doctrine in *Red Lion Broadcasting Co. v. FCC*, 1969.)

When the Sinclair Broadcast Group retreated from pre-election plans to force its 62 television stations to preempt primetime programming in favor of airing the blatantly anti–John Kerry documentary *Stolen Honor: Wounds That Never Heal*, the reversal wasn't triggered by a concern for fairness: Sinclair back-pedaled because its stock was tanking. The staunchly conservative broadcaster's plan had provoked calls for sponsor boycotts, and Wall Street saw a company that was putting politics ahead of profits. Sinclair's stock declined by nearly 17 percent before the company announced it would air a somewhat more balanced news program in place of the documentary. (*Baltimore Sun*, 10/24/04).

But if fairness mattered little to Sinclair, the news that a corporation that controlled more TV licenses than any other could put the publicly owned airwaves to partisan use sparked discussion

"The Fairness Doctrine: How We Lost It and Why We Need It Back," by Steve Rendall, Fairness and Accuracy in Reporting (FAIR), January 1, 2005. Reprinted by permission.

of fairness across the board, from media democracy activists to television industry executives.

Variety (10/25/04) underlined industry concerns in a report suggesting that Sinclair's partisanship was making other broadcasters nervous by fueling "anti-consolidation forces" and efforts to bring back the FCC's defunct Fairness Doctrine:

> Sinclair could even put the Fairness Doctrine back in play, a rule established in 1949 to require that the networks—all three of them—air all sides of issues. The doctrine was abandoned in the 1980s with the proliferation of cable, leaving citizens with little recourse over broadcasters that misuse the public airwaves, except to oppose the renewal of licenses.

The Sinclair controversy brought discussion of the Fairness Doctrine back to news columns (*Baltimore Sun*, 10/24/04; *L.A. Times*, 10/24/04) and opinion pages (*Portland Press Herald*, 10/24/04; *Fort Worth Star-Telegram*, 10/22/04) across the country. *Legal Times* (11/15/04) weighed in with an in-depth essay headlined: "A Question of Fair Air Play: Can Current Remedies for Media Bias Handle Threats Like Sinclair's Aborted Anti-Kerry Program?"

Sinclair's history of one-sided editorializing and right-wing water-carrying, which long preceded its *Stolen Honor* ploy (*Extra!*, 11–12/04), puts it in the company of political talk radio, where right-wing opinion is the rule, locally and nationally. Together, they are part of a growing trend that sees movement conservatives and Republican partisans using the publicly owned airwaves as a political megaphone—one that goes largely unanswered by any regular opposing perspective. It's an imbalance that begs for a remedy.

A Short History of Fairness

The necessity for the Fairness Doctrine, according to proponents, arises from the fact that there are many fewer broadcast licenses than people who would like to have them. Unlike publishing, where the tools of the trade are in more or less endless supply, broadcasting licenses are limited by the finite number of available frequencies. Thus, as trustees of a scarce public resource, licensees accept certain public interest obligations in exchange for the exclusive use of limited public airwaves. One such obligation was the Fairness Doctrine, which was meant to ensure that a variety of views, beyond those of the licensees and those they favored, were heard on the airwaves. (Since cable's infrastructure is privately owned and cable channels can, in theory, be endlessly multiplied, the FCC does not put public interest requirements on that medium.)

The Fairness Doctrine had two basic elements: It required broadcasters to devote some of their airtime to discussing controversial matters of public interest, and to air contrasting views regarding those matters. Stations were given wide latitude as to how to provide contrasting views: It could be done through news segments, public affairs shows or editorials.

Formally adopted as an FCC rule in 1949 and repealed in 1987 by Ronald Reagan's pro-broadcaster FCC, the doctrine can be traced back to the early days of broadcast regulation.

Early on, legislators wrestled over competing visions of the future of radio: Should it be commercial or non-commercial? There was even a proposal by the U.S. Navy to control the new technology. The debate included early arguments about how to address the public interest, as well as fears about the awesome power conferred on a handful of licensees.

> American thought and American politics will be largely at the mercy of those who operate these stations, for publicity is the most powerful weapon that can be wielded in a republic. And when such a weapon is placed in the hands of one person, or a single selfish group is permitted to either tacitly or otherwise acquire ownership or dominate these broadcasting stations throughout the country, then woe be to those who dare to differ with them. It will be impossible to compete with them in reaching the ears of the American people.
>
> — Rep. Luther Johnson (D.-Texas), in the debate that preceded the Radio Act of 1927 (KPFA, 1/16/03)

In the Radio Act of 1927, Congress mandated the FCC's forerunner, the Federal Radio Commission (FRC), to grant broadcasting licenses in such a manner as to ensure that licensees served the "public convenience, interest or necessity."

As former FCC commissioner Nicholas Johnson pointed out (*California Lawyer*, 8/88), it was in that spirit that the FRC, in 1928, first gave words to a policy formulation that would become known as the Fairness Doctrine, calling for broadcasters to show "due regard for the opinions of others." In 1949, the FCC adopted the doctrine as a formal rule (FCC, Report on Editorializing by Broadcast Licensees, 1949).

In 1959 Congress amended the Communications Act of 1934 to enshrine the Fairness Doctrine into law, rewriting Chapter 315(a) to read: "A broadcast licensee shall afford reasonable opportunity for discussion of conflicting views on matters of public importance."

> It is the purpose of the First Amendment to preserve an uninhibited marketplace of ideas in which truth will ultimately prevail, rather than to countenance monopolization of that market, whether it be by the government itself or a private licensee. It is the right of the public to receive suitable access to social, political, aesthetic, moral and other ideas and experiences which is crucial here. That right may not constitutionally be abridged either by Congress or by the FCC.
>
> — U.S. Supreme Court, *Red Lion Broadcasting Co. v. FCC*, 1969.

A decade later the United States Supreme Court upheld the doctrine's constitutionality in *Red Lion Broadcasting Co. v. FCC* (1969), foreshadowing a decade in which the FCC would view the Fairness Doctrine as a guiding principle, calling it "the single most important requirement of operation in the public interest—the sine qua non for grant of a renewal of license" (FCC Fairness Report, 1974).

How It Worked

There are many misconceptions about the Fairness Doctrine. For instance, it did not require that each program be internally balanced, nor did it mandate equal time for opposing points of view. And it didn't require that the balance of a station's program lineup be anything like 50/50.

Nor, as Rush Limbaugh has repeatedly claimed, was the Fairness Doctrine all that stood between conservative talkshow hosts and the dominance they would attain after the doctrine's repeal. In fact, not one Fairness Doctrine decision issued by the FCC had ever concerned itself with talk shows. Indeed, the talk show format was born and flourished while the doctrine was in operation. Before the doctrine was repealed, right-wing hosts frequently dominated talk show schedules, even in liberal cities, but none was ever muzzled (*The Way Things Aren't*, Rendall et al., 1995). The Fairness Doctrine simply prohibited stations from broadcasting from a single perspective, day after day, without presenting opposing views.

In answer to charges, put forward in the Red Lion case, that the doctrine violated broadcasters' First Amendment free speech rights because the government was exerting editorial control, Supreme Court Justice Byron White wrote: "There is no sanctuary in the First Amendment for unlimited private censorship operating in a medium not open to all." In a *Washington Post* column (1/31/94), the Media Access Project (MAP), a telecommunications law firm that supports the Fairness Doctrine, addressed the First Amendment issue: "The Supreme Court unanimously found [the Fairness Doctrine] advances First Amendment values. It safeguards the public's right to be informed on issues affecting our democracy, while also balancing broadcasters' rights to the broadest possible editorial discretion."

Indeed, when it was in place, citizen groups used the Fairness Doctrine as a tool to expand speech and debate. For instance, it prevented stations from allowing only one side to be heard on ballot measures. Over the years, it had been supported by grassroots groups across the political spectrum, including the ACLU, National Rifle Association and the right-wing Accuracy In Media.

Typically, when an individual or citizens group complained to a station about imbalance, the station would set aside time for an on-air response for the omitted perspective: "Reasonable opportunity for presentation of opposing points of view," was the relevant phrase. If a station disagreed with the complaint, feeling that an adequate range of views had already been presented, the decision would be appealed to the FCC for a judgment.

According to Andrew Jay Schwartzman, president of MAP, scheduling response time was based on time of day, frequency and duration of the original perspective. "If one view received a lot of coverage in primetime," Schwartzman told *Extra!*, "then at least some response time would have to be in primetime. Likewise if one side received many short spots or really long spots." But the remedy did not amount to equal time; the ratio of airtime between the original perspective and the response "could be as much as five to one," said Schwartzman.

As a guarantor of balance and inclusion, the Fairness Doctrine was no panacea. It was somewhat vague, and depended on the vigilance of listeners and viewers to notice imbalance. But its value, beyond the occasional remedies it provided, was in its codification of the principle that broadcasters had a responsibility to present a range of views on controversial issues.

The Doctrine's Demise

From the 1920s through the '70s, the history of the Fairness Doctrine paints a picture of public servants wrestling with how to maintain some public interest standards in the operation of publicly owned—but corporate-dominated—airwaves. Things were about to change.

The 1980s brought the Reagan Revolution, with its army of anti-regulatory extremists; not least among these was Reagan's new FCC chair, Mark S. Fowler. Formerly a broadcast industry lawyer, Fowler earned his reputation as "the James Watt of the FCC" by sneering at the notion that broadcasters had a unique role or bore special responsibilities to ensure democratic discourse (*California Lawyer*, 8/88). It was all nonsense, said Fowler (*L.A. Times*, 5/1/03): "The perception of broadcasters as community trustees should be replaced by a view of broadcasters as marketplace participants." To Fowler, television was "just another appliance—it's a toaster with pictures," and he seemed to endorse total deregulation (*Washington Post*, 2/6/83): "We've got to look beyond the conventional wisdom that we must somehow regulate this box."

Of course, Fowler and associates didn't favor total deregulation: Without licensing, the airwaves would descend into chaos as many broadcasters competed for the same frequencies, a situation that would mean ruin for the traditional corporate broadcasters they were so close to. But regulation for the public good rather than corporate convenience was deemed suspect.

Fowler vowed to see the Fairness Doctrine repealed, and though he would depart the commission a few months before the goal was realized, he worked assiduously at setting the stage for the doctrine's demise.

He and his like-minded commissioners, a majority of whom had been appointed by President Ronald Reagan, argued that the doctrine violated broadcasters' First Amendment free speech rights by giving government a measure of editorial control over stations. Moreover, rather than increase debate and discussion of controversial issues, they argued, the doctrine actually chilled debate, because stations feared demands for response time and possible challenges to broadcast licenses (though only one license was ever revoked in a dispute involving the Fairness Doctrine—*California Lawyer*, 8/88).

The FCC stopped enforcing the doctrine in the mid-'80s, well before it formally revoked it. As much as the commission majority wanted to repeal the doctrine outright, there was one hurdle that stood between them and their goal: Congress' 1959 amendment to the Communications Act had made the doctrine law.

Help would come in the form of a controversial 1986 legal decision by Judge Robert Bork and then-Judge Antonin Scalia, both Reagan appointees on the D.C. Circuit of the U.S. Court of Appeals. Their 2-1 opinion avoided the constitutional issue altogether, and simply declared that Congress had not actually made the doctrine into a law. Wrote Bork: "We do not believe that language adopted in 1959 made the Fairness Doctrine a binding statutory obligation," because, he said, the doctrine was imposed "under," not "by" the Communications Act of 1934 (*California Lawyer*, 8/88). Bork held that the 1959 amendment established that the FCC could apply the doctrine, but was not obliged to do so—that keeping the rule or scuttling it was simply a matter of FCC discretion.

"The decision contravened 25 years of FCC holdings that the doctrine had been put into law in 1959," according to MAP. But it signaled the end of the Fairness Doctrine, which was repealed in 1987 by the FCC under new chair Dennis R. Patrick, a lawyer and Reagan White House aide.

A year after the doctrine's repeal, writing in *California Lawyer* (8/88), former FCC commissioner Johnson summed up the fight to bring back the Fairness Doctrine as "a struggle for nothing less than possession of the First Amendment: Who gets to have and express opinions in America." Though a bill before Congress to reinstate the doctrine passed overwhelmingly later that year, it failed to override Reagan's veto. Another attempt to resurrect the doctrine in 1991 ran out of steam when President George H. W. Bush threatened another veto.

Where Things Stand

What has changed since the repeal of the Fairness Doctrine? Is there more coverage of controversial issues of public importance? "Since the demise of the Fairness Doctrine we have had much less coverage of issues," says MAP's Schwartzman, adding that television news and public affairs programming has decreased locally and nationally. According to a study conducted by MAP and the Benton Foundation, 25 percent of broadcast stations no longer offer any local news or public affairs programming at all (*Federal Communications Law Journal*, 5/03).

The most extreme change has been in the immense volume of unanswered conservative opinion heard on the airwaves, especially on talk radio. Nationally, virtually all of the leading political talk show hosts are right-wingers: Rush Limbaugh, Sean Hannity, Michael Savage, Oliver North, G. Gordon Liddy, Bill O'Reilly and Michael Reagan, to name just a few. The same goes for local talk shows. One product of the post-Fairness era is the conservative "Hot Talk" format, featuring one right-wing host after another and little else. Disney-owned KSFO in liberal San Francisco is one such station (*Extra!*, 3-4/95). Some towns have two.

When Edward Monks, a lawyer in Eugene, Oregon, studied the two commercial talk stations in his town (*Eugene Register-Guard*, 6/30/02), he found "80 hours per week, more than 4,000 hours per year, programmed for Republican and conservative talk shows, without a single second programmed for a Democratic or liberal perspective." Observing that Eugene (a generally progressive town) was "fairly representative," Monks concluded: "Political opinions expressed on talk radio are approaching the level of uniformity that would normally be achieved only in a totalitarian society. There is nothing fair, balanced or democratic about it."

Bringing Back Fairness?

For citizens who value media democracy and the public interest, broadcast regulation of our publicly owned airwaves has reached a low-water mark. In his new book, *Crimes Against Nature*, Robert F. Kennedy Jr. probes the failure of broadcasters to cover the environment, writing, "The FCC's pro-industry, anti-regulatory philosophy has effectively ended the right of access to broadcast television by any but the moneyed interests."

According to *TV Week* (11/30/04), a coalition of broadcast giants is currently pondering a legal assault on the Supreme Court's *Red Lion* decision. "Media General and a coalition of major TV network owners—NBC Universal, News Corp. and Viacom—made clear that they are seriously considering an attack on *Red Lion* as part of an industry challenge to an appellate court decision scrapping FCC media ownership deregulation earlier this year."

Considering the many looming problems facing media democracy advocates, *Extra!* asked MAP's Schwartzman why activists should still be concerned about the Fairness Doctrine:

> What has not changed since 1987 is that over-the-air broadcasting remains the most powerful force affecting public opinion, especially on local issues; as public trustees, broadcasters ought to be insuring that they inform the public, not inflame them. That's why we need a Fairness Doctrine. It's not a universal solution. It's not a substitute for reform or for diversity of ownership. It's simply a mechanism to address the most extreme kinds of broadcast abuse.

Chapter 2

Are Media Conglomerates to Blame for a Lack of Trust in Traditional Media?

Overview: Who Owns Your News?

OpenStax, Rice University

OpenStax is a nonprofit educational technology initiative based at Rice University. Since 2012, OpenStax has created peer-reviewed, openly licensed textbooks, which are available in free digital formats and for a low cost in print.

What started as print (media) journalism was subsequently supplemented by radio coverage, then network television, followed by cable television. Now, with the addition of the Internet, blogs and social media—a set of applications or web platforms that allow users to immediately communicate with one another—give citizens a wide variety of sources for instant news of all kinds. The Internet also allows citizens to initiate public discussion by uploading images and video for viewing, such as videos documenting interactions between citizens and the police, for example. Provided we are connected digitally, we have a bewildering amount of choices for finding information about the world. In fact, some might say that compared to the tranquil days of the 1970s, when we might read the morning newspaper over breakfast and take in the network news at night, there are now too many choices in today's increasingly complex world of information. This reality may make the news media all the more important to structuring and shaping narratives about U.S. politics. The proliferation of competing information sources like blogs and social media may actually weaken the power of the news media relative to the days when news media monopolized our attention.

The term *media* defines a number of different communication formats from television media, which share information through broadcast airwaves, to print media, which rely on printed documents. The collection of all forms of media that communicate information to the general public is called mass media, including television, print, radio, and Internet. One of the primary reasons citizens turn to the media is for news. We expect the media to cover important political and social events and information in a concise and neutral manner.

To accomplish its work, the media employs a number of people in varied positions. Journalists and reporters are responsible for uncovering news stories by keeping an eye on areas of public interest, like politics, business, and sports. Once a journalist has a lead or a possible idea for a story, he or she researches background information and interviews people to create a complete and balanced account. Editors work in the background of the newsroom, assigning stories, approving articles or packages, and editing content for accuracy and clarity. Publishers are people or companies that own and produce print or digital media. They oversee both the content and finances of the publication, ensuring the organization turns a profit and creates a high-quality product to distribute to consumers. Producers oversee the production and finances of visual media, like television, radio, and film.

The work of the news media should differ from public relations, which is communication carried out to improve the image of companies, organizations, or candidates for office. Public relations is not a neutral information form, and accusations abound against media outlets acting as partisan promoters rather than ethically neutral journalists. While journalists write stories to inform the public, a public relations spokesperson helps an individual or organization get positive press. Public relations materials normally appear as press releases or paid advertisements in newspapers and other media outlets. Some less reputable publications, however, publish paid articles under the news banner, blurring the line between journalism and public relations.

Media Types

Each form of media has its own complexities and is used by different demographics.

Television alone offers viewers a variety of formats. Programming may be scripted, like dramas or comedies, or unscripted, like game shows or reality programs, or informative, such as news programming. Most local stations are affiliated with a national network corporation, and they broadcast national network programming to their local viewers.

Before the existence of cable and fiber optics, networks needed to own local affiliates to have access to the local station's transmission towers. Towers have a limited radius, so each network needed an affiliate in each major city to reach viewers. While cable technology has lessened networks' dependence on aerial signals, some viewers still use antennas and receivers to view programming broadcast from local towers.

Affiliates, by agreement with the networks, give priority to network news and other programming chosen by the affiliate's national media corporation. Local affiliate stations are told when to air programs or commercials, and they diverge only to inform the public about a local or national emergency.

Most affiliate stations will show local news before and after network programming to inform local viewers of events and issues. Network news has a national focus on politics, international events, the economy, and more. Local news, on the other hand, is likely to focus on matters close to home, such as regional business, crime, sports, and weather.[1]

Cable programming offers national networks a second method to directly reach local viewers. As the name implies, cable stations transmit programming directly to a local cable company hub, which then sends the signals to homes through coaxial or fiber optic cables. Because cable does not broadcast programming through the airwaves, cable networks can operate across the nation directly without local affiliates. Instead they purchase broadcasting rights for the cable stations they believe their viewers want. For this reason, cable networks often specialize in different types of programming.

The on-demand nature of the Internet has created many opportunities for news outlets. Unfortunately, the proliferation of online news has also increased the amount of poorly written material with little editorial oversight, and readers must be cautious when reading Internet news sources. Even large news outlets, like the Associated Press, have published articles with errors in their haste to get a story out.

The Internet also facilitates the flow of information through social media, which allows users to instantly communicate with one another and share with audiences that can grow exponentially. Social media changes more rapidly than the other media formats. A growing number of these sites also allow users to comment anonymously, leading to increases in threats and abuse. The site 4chan, for example, was linked to the 2015 shooting at an Oregon community college.[2]

Regardless of where we get our information, the various media avenues available today, versus years ago, make it much easier for everyone to be engaged. The question is: Who controls the media we rely on? Most media are controlled by a limited number of conglomerates. A conglomerate is a corporation made up of a number of companies, organizations, and media networks. In the 1980s, more than fifty companies owned the majority of television and radio stations and networks. Now, only six conglomerates control most of the broadcast media in the United States: CBS Corporation, Comcast, Time Warner, 21st Century Fox (formerly News Corporation), Viacom, and The Walt Disney Company.[3]

The Walt Disney Company, for example, owns the ABC Television Network, ESPN, A&E, and Lifetime, in addition to the Disney Channel. Viacom owns BET, Comedy Central, MTV, Nickelodeon, and Vh2. Time Warner owns Cartoon Network, CNN, HBO, and TNT, among others. While each of these networks has its own programming, in the end, the conglomerate can make a policy that affects all stations and programming under its control.

Conglomerates can create a monopoly on information by controlling a sector of a market. When a media conglomerate has policies or restrictions, they will apply to all stations or outlets under its ownership, potentially limiting the information citizens receive. Conglomerate ownership also creates circumstances in which censorship may occur.

Newspapers too have experienced the pattern of concentrated ownership. Gannett Company, while also owning television media, holds a large number of newspapers and news magazines in its control. Many of these were acquired quietly, without public notice or discussion. Gannett's 2013 acquisition of publishing giant A.H. Belo Corporation caused some concern and news coverage, however. The sale would have allowed Gannett to own both an NBC and a CBS affiliate in St. Louis, Missouri, giving it control over programming and advertising rates for two competing stations. The U.S. Department of Justice required Gannett to sell the station owned by Belo to ensure market competition and multi-ownership in St. Louis.[4]

These changes in the format and ownership of media raise the question whether the media still operate as an independent source of information. Is it possible that corporations and CEOs now control the information flow, making profit more important than the impartial delivery of information? The reality is that media outlets, whether newspaper, television, radio, or Internet, are businesses. They have expenses and must raise revenues. At the same time, we expect the media to entertain, inform, and alert us without bias. The media may also serve as a point of access for the public. The media must provide some public services, while following laws and regulations. Reconciling these goals may not always be possible.

Functions of the Media

The media exist to fill a number of functions. Whether the medium is a newspaper, a radio, or a television newscast, a corporation behind the scenes must bring in revenue and pay for the cost of the product. Revenue comes from advertising and sponsors. Corporations will not pay for advertising if there are no viewers or readers.

The media should also function as watchdogs of society and of public officials. Some refer to the media as the fourth estate, with the branches of government being the first three estates and the media equally participating as the fourth. This role helps maintain the republic and keeps the government accountable for its actions, even if a branch of the government is reluctant to open itself to public scrutiny. As much as social scientists would like citizens to be informed and involved in politics and events, the reality is that we are not. So the media, especially journalists, keep an eye on what is happening and sounds an alarm when the public needs to pay attention.[5]

The media also engages in agenda setting, which is the act of choosing which issues or topics deserve public discussion. For example, in the early 1980s, famine in Ethiopia drew worldwide attention, which resulted in increased charitable giving to the country. Yet the famine had been going on for a long time before it was discovered by western media. Even after the discovery, it took video footage to gain the attention of the British and U.S. populations and start the aid flowing.[6]

Today, numerous examples of agenda setting show how important the media are when trying to prevent further emergencies or humanitarian crises. In the spring of 2015, when the Dominican Republic was preparing to exile Haitians and undocumented (or under documented) residents, major U.S. news outlets remained silent. However, once the story had been covered several times by Al Jazeera, a state-funded broadcast company based in Qatar, ABC, the *New York Times*, and other network outlets followed.[7] With major network coverage came public pressure for the U.S. government to act on behalf of the Haitians.[8]

Before the Internet, traditional media determined whether citizen photographs or video footage would become "news." In 1991, a private citizen's camcorder footage showed four police officers beating an African American motorist named Rodney King in Los Angeles. After appearing on local independent television station, KTLA-TV, and then the national news, the event began a national discussion on police brutality and ignited riots in Los Angeles.[9]

The agenda-setting power of traditional media is often appropriated by social media and smartphones. Tumblr, Facebook, YouTube, and other Internet sites allow witnesses to instantly upload images and accounts of events and forward the link to friends. Some uploads go viral and attract the attention of the mainstream media, but large network newscasts and major newspapers are still more powerful at initiating or changing a discussion.

While journalists reporting the news try to present information in an unbiased fashion, sometimes they put forth opinions and analysis of complicated issues.

Notes

1. Jeremy Lipschultz and Michael Hilt. 2003. "Race and Local Television News Crime Coverage," *Studies in Media & Information Literacy Education* 3, No. 4: 1–10.
2. Daniel Marans, "Did the Oregon Shooter Warn of His Plans on 4chan?" *Huffington Post*, 1 October 2015.
3. Vanna Le, "Global 2000: The World's Largest Media Companies of 2014," *Forbes*, 7 May 2014.
4. Meg James, "DOJ Clears Gannett-Belo Deal but Demands Sale of St. Louis TV Station," *Los Angeles Times*, 16 December 2013.
5. John Zaller. 2003. "A New Standard of News Quality: Burglar Alarms for the Monitorial Citizen," *Political Communication* 20, No. 2: 109–130.
6. Suzanne Ranks, "Ethiopian Famine: How Landmark BBC Report Influenced Modern Coverage," *Guardian*, 22 October 2014.
7. Hisham Aidi, "Haitians in the Dominican Republic in Legal Limbo," Al Jazeera, 10 April 2015.
8. "Pressure the Government of the Dominican Republic to Stop Its Planned 'Cleaning' of 250,000 Black Dominicans," https://petitions.whitehouse.gov/petition/pressure-government-dominican-republic-stop-its-planned-cleaning-250000-black-dominicans (November 26, 2015); Led Black, "Prevent Humanitarian Tragedy in Dominican Republic," CNN, 23 June 2015.
9. Erik Ortiz, "George Holliday, Who Taped Rodney King Beating, Urges Others to Share Videos," NBC, 9 June 2015.

Advertising Revenue Has an Impact on Media Reporting

Graham Beattie, Ruben Durante, Brian Knight, and Ananya Sen

Graham Beattie is an assistant professor in the Department of Economics at Loyola Marymount University. Ruben Durante is a full professor of economics and ICREA researcher at Universitat Pompeu Fabra in Barcelona, and associate researcher of the Institute of Political Economy and Governance (IPEG) and of the Barcelona School of Economics (BSE). Brian Knight is a professor of economics at Brown University, vice chair of the Economics Department, and a research associate at the National Bureau of Economic Research. Ananya Sen is an assistant professor at Carnegie Mellon University's Heinz College.

An independent media sector is essential for the provision of information about issues of consequence, ranging from policy to government performance to corporate misconduct. However, this role for the media creates incentives for powerful interests, such as large corporations, to attempt to sway coverage in their favor. Advertising, which can be used as a lever to pressure news outlets to suppress negative stories, is one of the primary tools for corporations. In the face of potentially negative news about their advertisers, media outlets might suppress stories in order to maintain their relationship with those companies.

This form of media bias is particularly salient because media outlets are primarily advertiser-funded. Moreover, over the past two decades, digitization has disrupted traditional advertising-based business models, making news outlets even more reliant

Republished with permission of INFORMS, from G. Beattie, R. Durante, B. Knight, and A. Sen (2021). "Advertising spending and media bias: Evidence from news coverage of car safety recalls." *Management Science* 67(2):698-719; permission conveyed through Copyright Clearance Center, Inc.

on their remaining advertisers. This potential for advertiser-based media bias has received little attention in the academic literature, which has focused more on the impact of corporate and government ownership of news outlets and its impact on coverage. Advertising-based media bias is perhaps more insidious since consumers might not be able to identify these potential conflicts of interest and the resulting bias in coverage. While there is some anecdotal evidence of such bias, there is limited systematic empirical evidence of this phenomenon.

Causal identification of the impact of advertising revenue on coverage decisions is challenging because the media section is a quintessential two-sided market. That is, media outlets face incentives to report on stories that cater to the tastes of their consumers. At the same time, firms have an incentive to advertise in media outlets with consumers who have a taste for their product. Thus, a correlation between advertising and favorable coverage could be driven by this coverage attracting consumers and these consumers attracting advertisers.

In "Advertising Spending and Media Bias: Evidence from News Coverage of Car Safety Recalls," Graham Beattie, Ruben Durante, Brian Knight and Ananya Sen attempt to overcome this challenge by analyzing newspaper coverage of car safety recalls. In this case, the preferences of readers should be diametrically opposed to those of car manufacturers who advertise in the newspaper. In particular, consumers demand more safety-related information and in particular for the manufacturers and models that they own or are considering purchasing. Car manufacturers want to advertise to the consumers most interested in their products but also want to minimize negative coverage that might adversely affect their brand. The authors carry out a large-scale study in this setting, analyzing over 100 newspapers in the United States over a 15-year period. They focus on how newspapers cover car safety recalls, linking coverage to newspaper-specific advertising revenue from the manufacturer involved in the recall.

The authors document that newspapers bias their coverage in favor of car manufacturers that have advertised with them. In particular, newspapers reduce their negative coverage of the manufacturer's recall event more for manufacturers that have more advertising spending over the previous two years. This effect exists despite consumer-driven pressures pushing coverage in the opposite direction, as recalls are covered more in Metropolitan Statistical Areas (MSAs) with higher rates of ownership of the recalled vehicle.

The effect of advertising on coverage is larger for advertising from national manufacturers in large newspapers than for advertising from local dealerships in small newspapers. Further, the effect is larger if advertising levels have been stable over the previous two years. Taken together, these findings suggest that advertising has the largest effect on newspaper coverage in cases in which there is a reliable relationship between advertiser and newspaper, likely because these relationships are most likely to continue to be lucrative if the newspaper stays in the good graces of the advertiser.

Beattie, Durante, Knight, and Sen also investigate competition between newspapers in order to assess the role of market structure in media bias. Using variation in the number of newspapers that serve an area, they find that higher levels of competition lead to lower levels of media bias, and the results are similar when analyzing newspaper exits. The paper also examines how digitization affects market structure. In particular, the introduction of Craigslist in newspaper markets increases the degree of bias towards advertisers. This implies that, as online platforms, such as Craigslist, take advertising revenue away from newspapers, newspapers become more reliant on their existing corporate advertisers and start biasing their coverage more in their favor.

The study sheds light on content strategies employed by platforms in an environment in which the preferences of different sides of the market are at odds with each other. It also highlights how these strategies evolve to deal with financial hardships brought on due to digitization over the past two decades. While some level of advertising-based media bias might be inevitable, the study does point to some crucial implications for policymakers, in particular the importance of competition between news outlets to limit the degree of any such bias.

The FCC's Hands-Off Approach to Media Consolidation Means That Local News Increasingly Looks More Like Fox News

Gregory J. Martin and Joshua McCrain

Gregory J. Martin is assistant professor of political economics at Stanford Graduate School of Business. His research focuses on political marketplaces, the political media consulting industry, and the allocation of grant funding by legislatures. Joshua McCrain is a graduate student in the Department of Political Science at Emory University. His research focuses on lobbying, Congress, media and politics, and political methodology.

The American news media landscape—much like the American political landscape in general—has become increasingly nationalized and ideologically polarized over the past two decades. A handful of large national papers are growing readership and expanding their coverage, while nearly 1800 local newspapers have closed since 2004. On television, the trends are less steep but point in the same direction: local news viewership is in slow decline, while ideologically polarized national cable TV outlets gain viewers.

It's possible that these trends simply reflect adaptation by the news industry to changes in Americans' tastes for political information. In an age of increasing nationalization of elections, dedicated coverage of local politics may no longer be as valuable to citizens as it once was.

Our research investigated an alternative explanation: that these content shifts are driven not by outlets giving consumers what they want, but by changes on the supply side of the news market. The media industry experienced a wave of ownership consolidation

"The FCC's Hands-Off Approach to Media Consolidation Means That Local News Increasingly Looks More Like Fox News," by Gregory J. Martin and Joshua McCrain, London School of Economics. Reprinted by permission.

that began in the 1980s but reached a crest in recent years. This consolidation trend was especially stark on television: by 2017, just five companies owned nearly 40 percent of full-power broadcast TV stations in the US.

We examined the consequences of an acquisition by the largest of these companies, the Sinclair Broadcast Group. In the summer of 2017, Sinclair purchased 14 local television stations previously owned by the Bonten Group. We examined what happened to the content and viewership of the local news broadcasts on these stations, and their competitors in the same media markets, before and after the acquisition. To do this, we collected a database of roughly 7.4 million transcript segments from local news programs across the country, along with information about local news viewership at 743 local stations.

We found that the acquisition led to a roughly 25 percent increase in the share of news programming devoted to coverage of national politics at the acquired stations. This increase came largely at the expense of coverage of local politics, which declined by a similar amount. We also found that a measure of ideological "slant" based on the content of news segments shifted to the right at Sinclair-acquired stations following the acquisition, compared to other stations in the same market. Following the acquisition, news programs on Sinclair-owned stations looked more like Fox News and less like MSNBC than they had before.

Viewers' reaction to these changes was negative: Sinclair-acquired stations experienced a small drop in viewership following the acquisition. The shifts toward a righter leaning slant and more national politics coverage do not appear to have gained these stations additional viewers. It is thus hard to explain the changes in content that Sinclair implemented as being primarily driven by a desire to cater to viewer tastes.

Why did Sinclair implement these changes in content, if not to increase viewership and thereby its ad revenues? We posit an explanation driven by economies of scale in the production of news by a conglomerate owner. An owner of many stations operating in many markets like Sinclair can reduce production costs, perhaps dramatically, by substituting nationally-focused and ideologically unified content produced in a single studio for locally-focused and ideologically diverse content produced by many local journalists. Even if viewers don't like this change—and they appear not to—the cost savings could still dominate in Sinclair's thinking.

Media consolidation is therefore not neutral with respect to the content of news coverage. Consolidation changes the incentives of news providers, shifting coverage towards topics that can be distributed in multiple markets rather than those—such as local politics—that are market-specific.

Our results have strong implications for the regulatory oversight of mergers in the TV industry. One factor enabling Sinclair's rapid recent expansion was the Federal Communication Commission's (FCC) elimination of the "main studio rule," which required local news stations to maintain a physical studio in the broadcast area. The elimination of this rule increased the cost efficiencies of consolidation, encouraging a wave of mergers. Our findings document a cost of the current hands-off approach to cross-market consolidation.

Regulatory oversight has traditionally focused on measures of concentration defined at the local market level; for example, the FCC caps the fraction of stations in a single market that can be owned by the same company. Our analysis shows that such market-level concentration analysis is insufficient: the news content that would be provided by a TV industry consisting of a handful of national conglomerates would look very different than that provided by one comprising numerous single-market operators, even holding measures of market-level concentration fixed.

Given the importance of local news provision for the accountability of local elected officials, regulators should not neglect this effect of cross-market ownership consolidation on local news content. Current trends towards national consolidation in TV and other media ownership have worrying implications for the performance of local governments and for mass polarization.

Media Consolidation Is a Troubling, Even Dangerous, Trend

Margot Susca

Margot Susca, Ph.D., is an assistant professor in the journalism division at American University whose work operates at the intersection of investigative journalism and critical communications research, specifically focused on corporate media ownership and democracy and guided by the principles of the political economy of media.

In the U.S., only a handful of media companies control what children and adults watch and read.

Now that number could get even smaller.

The proposed US$52.4 billion merger of Disney and 21st Century Fox would merge the first and third largest film companies in the world. Marvel Studios, Lucasfilm, Pixar, Searchlight, 20th Century Fox and Big Sky would all be under the same umbrella. Disney would also acquire control of TV channels like FX and National Geographic, adding to a portfolio that already includes ABC and ESPN. It would have majority stake in Hulu, which would position the streaming service to take on Netflix head-to-head in what many industry insiders expect will be a battle for market control.

As someone who studies global media power, I find the potential Disney-Fox merger troubling not just because one corporation will control production of narratives about popular culture and politics on television, film and streaming services, but because it will also create a media powerhouse worth so much that it could be as powerful as a state actor on the world stage.

"Disney's Potential 21st Century Fox Merger Continues Troubling Trend of Media Consolidation," by Margot Susca, The Conversation, December 21, 2017. https://theconversation.com/disneys-potential-21st-century-fox-merger-continues-troubling-trend-of-media-consolidation-89229.

"Weapons of Mass Distraction"

For children and adults, media isn't just entertainment. It is, in many ways, the tapestry of American life.

We grow up in front of the television screen, the silver screen and the computer screen, spending in the United States an astounding 12 hours daily engaged with media. It shapes our attitudes and beliefs, our likes and dislikes, our wants and desires and even our basic definitions of what it means to be normal.

Studies have found that Americans' attitudes about everything from terrorism to race relations are largely formed by what they watch and hear. For example, a 2015 study was able to show that negative stereotyping of Muslims in news reports led to increased support for military action against Muslim countries.

Meanwhile, fictional television shows like *Homeland*, *The Americans* and *24* routinely cast foreigners as villains, making it easier for audiences to demonize citizens from other countries and immigrants. These attitudes have been shown to have a real effect on public policy.

Advertising to children is a $17 billion industry. According to the Campaign for a Commercial Free Childhood, children's ads have all been connected to "eating disorders, precocious sexuality, youth violence and family stress," while contributing to "children's diminished capability to play creatively."

As is the case with all businesses, the bottom line for media companies trumps any consideration of the public good. Studios ultimately produce shows that attract the most viewers and sell the most ads and movie tickets: cheaply produced reality television, celebrity gossip, political drama, and films packed with action and special effects.

The result is a media system that has become what media scholar Marty Kaplan calls a "weapon of mass distraction."

A Consolidation Frenzy

Media control, then, has powerful implications in our society: The stories that appear influence how citizens make sense of the world.

When journalist and media critic Ben Bagdikian wrote his 1983 book *The Media Monopoly*, 50 companies controlled a majority of what Americans watched, read and heard.

Bagdikian predicted that further media consolidation of ownership would weaken coverage of lobbying, environmental issues, war, labor fights and corporate wrongdoing.

By the time he wrote his sequel in 2004, Bagdikian's predictions had largely come true. But even he didn't think that 90 percent of American media outlets would fall under the control of just five big media corporations. He wrote that these conglomerates operated as a kind of cartel that controlled our "most important institutions," from newspapers to film.

Disney, of course, was one of the five media conglomerates Bagdikian named. Another was Rupert Murdoch's News Corp., which, at the time, included parts of what would become 21st Century Fox.

Money Talks

If the $52 billion price tag sounds big, consider this: The payoff will be massive. The hybrid corporation control will give Disney a third of all domestic box office revenue, which, in 2017, amounted to about $3 billion.

Because the deal further shrinks the dwindling number of voices controlling media, Disney's merger with Fox has a long way to go to pass Department of Justice muster. Three major anti-trust laws are supposed to guide Department of Justice principles related to mergers and the resulting market conditions left in their wake.

But I expect we'll see what's happened in the past when regulators have attempted to control the ownership structure of other media conglomerates: a massive lobbying campaign. The $72 billion deal that merged Comcast and AT&T Broadband in 2001 was given the go-ahead. A decade later, Comcast bought NBC Universal for $30 billion, a merger that passed both FCC and Department of Justice scrutiny after being called a "lobbying frenzy" by Roll Call.

Disney already spends millions of dollars annually lobbying Congress, the U.S. State Department, the Federal Communications Commission and the Office of the U.S. Trade Representative, the federal agency responsible for negotiating with China to alter how it accepts and runs Hollywood films.

I also predict this merger will strengthen Disney's bargaining power with China, which controls film's release dates. China, the world's second-largest film market, typically blacks out American films during crucial summer blockbuster months to focus on domestic films, and it allows just 34 foreign films to be released each year. Yet some believe China will be more willing to negotiate with the mega-company that will emerge after the merger because of its sheer financial clout.

The merger, of course, will also influence what information reaches Americans, including content citizens need to govern themselves in a democracy.

Disney shares members of its board of directors with companies like Anheuser-Busch, Chase Manhattan, Coca-Cola, Unilever and Pfizer. Citizens should ask: How might this influence the information disseminated about food, banking regulations, consumer products and pharmaceuticals?

And consider how a stronger China-U.S. media alliance could impact U.S. films, television and news. Would American media companies be hesitant to cover human rights violations, factory conditions or pollution in Asia for fear that they would anger the Chinese government and, therefore, lose bargaining power and access to audiences?

What gets left out of coverage is sometimes as important as what makes it in.

If just four companies get to decide, we should all be concerned.

Corporate Giants Are Coming for Your Local News. Here's How We Fight Back.

Joseph Shieber

Joseph Shieber is associate professor of philosophy at Lafayette College. He previously taught philosophy at Brown University, the Massachusetts Institute of Technology, and Connecticut College. His research is primarily in the areas of epistemology, philosophy of language, and history of philosophy.

With two fell swoops recently, the twin dangers of media consolidation and news deserts are gathering new momentum—threatening the free flow of information, our civic discourse and our collective ability to make good decisions.

But it's not too late to do something about it. All of us can help reverse the steady deterioration of the free press by putting our wallets—and our votes—to work.

That isn't to say the task ahead will be easy. In fact, Alden Global Capital's new 32% stake in Tribune Media and the nearly $1.2 billion tie-up of newspaper behemoths Gannett and GateHouse Media—both unveiled in late November—underscore the long deregulation of media mergers.

The process began when the Federal Communications Commission started weakening restrictions on TV-station ownership in the 1980s. Since the 2000s, the trend has only accelerated: Fewer than 10 companies now control 90% of media outlets, down from 50 companies in 1983.

As for the newspaper industry, even before November, Gannett, GateHouse and Alden-owned Digital First Media were the three largest newspaper owners in the country, controlling more than 200 dailies. The 25 largest companies in the industry

"Corporate Giants Are Coming for Your Local News. Here's How We Fight Back," by Joseph Shieber, The Poynter Institute, February 5, 2020. Reprinted by permission.

own two-thirds of all U.S dailies—and the pre-merger Gannett and Digital First alone controlled around one-fifth of all dailies.

This corporate consolidation has led to an abandonment of local communities and a focus more on the company's short-term bottom line rather than on the long-term journalistic mission. The bottom-line orientation has gutted newspaper newsrooms, where overall employment fell by about 32,000 jobs nationwide from 2008 to 2017, according to federal figures. That's a nearly 45% decline.

Still, defenders of deregulation and consolidation cite the internet and how it's reshaped the media landscape. Apparently, if you don't like the news served by a corporate-controlled conglomerate, you are free to turn to "somebody sitting on their bed who weighs 400 pounds"—to borrow a phrase from President Donald Trump.

This is what demagogues like Russia's Vladimir Putin, Hungary's Viktor Orban and Turkey's Recep Erdogan want. It is no accident all three autocrats rose amid the hollowing-out of the media in their respective countries. Whether it's the Putin-instigated Russian invasion of Ukraine, Orban's nationalistic assault on minority rights in Hungary or Erdogan's attempt to wipe out the Syrian Kurds, demagoguery and corruption flourish when the public can no longer tell truth from lies.

Research bears this out. For example, in a working paper of the Hutchins Center at the Brookings Institution, researchers from Notre Dame and the University of Illinois Chicago established a causal relationship between the closure of local newspapers and higher borrowing costs for the municipalities that those papers served.

The researchers suggested that "local newspapers hold their governments accountable, keeping municipal borrowing costs low and ultimately saving local taxpayers money." That's why the rise of "news deserts" through the destruction of local media by corporate and private equity investors doesn't just hurt our civic discourse; it hurts our bottom line.

The path to a healthier public sphere demands an active media ecosystem in which journalistic professionals can thrive. Their norms include striving for objectivity, and more and more journalists understand that "objectivity" doesn't mean giving equal time to "both sides" but being true to the old-fashioned goal of getting the facts right. That's why we need to strengthen media organizations that put a premium on professional journalism and journalistic integrity.

Here are three concrete steps we can take to combat today's corporate media monoculture.

First, we can encourage elected leaders to take action. Bernie Sanders, Elizabeth Warren, Amy Klobuchar and Andrew Yang all have addressed the problems facing the news media. Sanders wants a moratorium on new media mergers, while Warren wants to regulate the private equity firms that are devastating the media landscape. These, plus ideas promoted by Yang and Klobuchar, are worth taking seriously.

Second, we can encourage those leaders to use the tools already in place to break up the largest media conglomerates. In 1945, the U.S. Supreme Court ruled in *Associated Press v. United States* that media organizations are subject to the antitrust laws governing other industries. In his decision, Justice Hugo Black noted that "the widest possible dissemination of information from diverse and antagonistic sources is essential to the welfare of the public [and] that a free press is a condition of a free society." The fact that the First Amendment guarantees "freedom of the press from governmental interference" does not mean that the government must "sanction repression of that freedom by private interests," Black wrote.

Third, we can support those independent media organizations around the country that are surviving—and, in many cases, thriving. Organizations like ProPublica, the Philadelphia Inquirer and the newspapers of the nonprofit-structured Independent Newsmedia Inc. are just some examples. You can learn more at savingcommunityjournalism.com, a resource associated with the

Center for Innovation and Sustainability in Local Media, at the University of North Carolina in Chapel Hill.

We as citizens will pay for it either way. Either we pay now for thriving, rigorously sourced journalism, or we'll pay with dysfunctional government and a debased civic discourse.

Journalists Should Reframe Their Reporting to Bolster Trust in Science

Denise-Marie Ordway

Denise-Marie Ordway is an award-winning journalist. She joined the Journalist's Resource in 2015 after working as a reporter for newspapers and radio stations in the US and Central America, including the Orlando Sentinel *and* Philadelphia Inquirer. *Her work also has appeared in publications such as* USA Today, *the* New York Times, *the* Chicago Tribune, *and the* Washington Post.

Journalists can bolster public trust in science if they present science as a process of exploration, scrutiny and self-correction instead of focusing on novel or sensational research and controversial retractions of published papers, a new study suggests.

Prior research has found that news stories about science in the U.S. tend to follow a few common themes, including characterizing science as being "broken" or "in crisis" and drawing attention to research retractions based on scientific misconduct, plagiarism or ethics violations.

The new study builds upon that research, finding that negative coverage of science without adequate context can erode public trust in scientists and induce negative beliefs about them. The study, "The Effects of Media Narratives About Failures and Discoveries in Science on Beliefs About and Support for Science," was published this month in the journal *Public Understanding of Science.*

Journalists need to change how they report on and frame scientific mistakes, according to the authors, Yotam Ophir, an assistant professor of communication at the University at Buffalo, State University of New York, and Kathleen Hall Jamieson, a

"By Changing Their Framing of Scientific Failures and Discoveries, Journalists Can Bolster Trust in Science: New Research," by Denise-Marie Ordway, The Journalist's Resource, May 27, 2021. https://journalistsresource.org/media/framing-scientific-errors-trust-science/.

communication professor and director of the University of Pennsylvania's Annenberg Public Policy Center.

Ophir says news outlets usually fail to recognize the role retractions play in advancing scientific knowledge. Discovering that findings from a peer-reviewed paper no longer hold true or that results cannot be replicated by other researchers is part of science's self-correction process.

Those important details are largely missing from news stories, he adds.

"Sure, talk about scientific failures—we want [journalists] to talk about scientific failures," Ophir says. "The public should know when scientific studies are successfully replicated and when they are not. But we also want journalists to remind their readers that that's how science works."

Jamieson says news coverage should emphasize that knowledge is provisional—research builds upon research over time.

"When something goes wrong in science and something gets retracted, the journalist has a choice about how to frame that retraction," Jamieson explains. "Those instances in which something really important was found and turned out to be an error—they are building blocks. They become the foundation for the knowledge move."

How They Did the Research

To gauge how news media accounts influence public perceptions of science, Ophir and Jamieson randomly assigned 4,497 U.S. adults to read one of five types of news articles. The articles were fabricated but based on real news coverage of science. Marketing research company Research Now recruited participants, who closely resembled the U.S. population in terms of age, gender, education and geographic region of residence.

Researchers assigned participants to four treatment conditions and one control condition, created for comparison purposes. People assigned to the control group read an article about baseball, chosen because the article's structure and length were similar to the science stories but on a topic unrelated to science.

Participants assigned to one of the treatment groups read stories about science built around narratives common in actual news coverage:

- Discovery: This type of coverage, the most prevalent of the four, "features terms such as 'advance,' 'path-breaking,' and 'breakthrough' and tells the story of scientists who have advanced knowledge through a finding cast as new and important, as a discovery," Ophir and Jamieson write in their paper. "These stories rarely acknowledge dead ends or false starts, and often fail to emphasize the need for additional ongoing research."
- The counterfeit quest: These news stories focus on a scientist or group of scientists "whose journey to 'discovery' and a resulting finding have been found wanting and purged from the scholarly record through retraction."
- Science is broken or in crisis: This narrative "concentrates not on individual scientists but on broader and more systemic problems in a specific scientific discipline or in science writ large." It draws attention to "a problem that science as an institution or collective community has ignored or downplayed."
- Problem explored: These stories spotlight "scientists exploring and hence potentially remedying one of the problems focal to the crisis or broken narrative."

After reading the articles, participants answered questions aimed at measuring their trust in scientists and their beliefs in areas such as whether science has benefited the U.S. and whether funding for science should be increased or reduced.

For example, people were asked to respond to the following prompts with a number ranging from 1 to 5, with 1 representing "rarely" and 5 representing "often:"

- "When a study is flawed, the scientists involved in it catch and correct the mistake prior to its publication."
- "When fraud occurs in scientific research, how often do you think it is caught?"

- "When scientists make mistakes in their research, how often do you think other scientists catch it?"

People assigned to read stories featuring the discovery theme expressed the strongest level of trust in scientists. Those who read stories indicating science is in crisis had the lowest.

Ophir and Jamieson also learned that people who expressed higher levels of trust were more likely to believe science is self-correcting—meaning that scholars continually uncover new ideas and evidence and build upon and correct older ones.

None of the story types had a statistically significant effect on opinions about whether science funding should rise or fall.

A Potential Solution

Ophir and Jamieson assert that news coverage featuring a problem-explored narrative can help the public understand that research findings are subject to ongoing scrutiny. The problem-explored narrative could "yield more positive beliefs and attitudes about science and scientists, by better communicating scientific norms of continuing exploration, scrutiny, and skepticism," they write in their paper.

The authors note that better science communication doesn't depend solely on journalists, however.

Scientists must make changes, too.

News coverage of science, they write, "is the product of a negotiation between scientists and journalists, both of which may be incentivized to prioritize more sensational, novel stories [at] the expense of the somewhat pedestrian, yet crucial, topic of self-correction."

Ophir and Jamieson add that "scientists and those who communicate about their findings need to develop narratives that reflect the nature of scientific inquiry and its norms and practices as well as the practices it uses to detect and correct error as well as fraud."

Censorship Practices Contribute to Mistrust of Media

Dan Sanchez

Dan Sanchez is the director of content at the Foundation for Economic Education (FEE) and the editor-in chief of FEE.org.

Soon, YouTubers will be silenced if they don't agree with the United Nations on public health. As *The Verdict* reports:

> YouTube will ban any content containing medical advice that contradicts World Health Organisation (WHO) coronavirus recommendations, according to CEO Susan Wojcicki.

Wojcicki announced the policy on CNN on Sunday. WHO is an agency of the UN, charged with overseeing global public health. *The Verdict* report continues:

> Wojcicki said that the Google-owned video streaming platform would be "removing information that is problematic."
>
> She told host Brian Stelter that this would include "anything that is medically unsubstantiated."
>
> "So people saying 'take vitamin C; take turmeric, we'll cure you,' those are the examples of things that would be a violation of our policy," she said.
>
> "Anything that would go against World Health Organisation recommendations would be a violation of our policy."
>
> While the decision has been welcomed by many, some have accused the streaming giant of censorship.

To be clear, for American YouTubers, this kind of censorship is not a violation of their constitutional right of free speech. The First Amendment protects citizens against *government* censorship, and

"YouTube to Ban Content That Contradicts WHO on COVID-19, Despite the UN Agency's Catastrophic Track Record of Misinformation," by Dan Sanchez, Foundation for Economic Education, April 23, 2020. https://fee.org/articles/youtube-to-ban-content-that-contradicts-who-on-covid-19-despite-the-un-agency-s-catastrophic-track-record-of-misinformation/.

YouTube is a private platform. Were the US government to force the private owners of YouTube to continue broadcasting certain videos against their will, that would be much more a violation of the First Amendment.

While YouTube's decision is not unconstitutional, it is unwise, exhibiting far too much deference to central authority in general and to WHO especially.

WHO's Track Record on the Issue

The World Health Organization is far from infallible. Its handling of information throughout the coronavirus emergency has been a long string of failures. As policy analyst Ross Marchand has recounted here on FEE last week, WHO failed to raise the alarm as the coronavirus rapidly spread through China during the crucial early period of the global crisis in January of this year. Then, as Marchand wrote:

> The global bureaucracy uncritically reported that Chinese authorities had seen "no clear evidence of human-to-human transmission of the novel coronavirus" on January 14, just one day after acknowledging the first case outside of China (in Thailand). WHO Director-General Dr. Tedros Adhanom Ghebreyesus praised Chinese President Xi Jinping for his "political commitment" and "political leadership" despite these repeated, reprehensible attempts to keep the world in the dark about the coronavirus.

President Donald Trump recently announced that the US would cease its funding of WHO over its many coronavirus-related failures.

And it is not just American conservatives who have been critical. As FEE's Jon Miltimore wrote a month ago:

> Our World in Data, an online publication based at the University of Oxford, announced on Tuesday that it had stopped relying on World Health Organization (WHO) data for its models, citing errors and other factors.

This raises an interesting question: would YouTube censor Oxford if it posted a video on the coronavirus issue with recommendations based on data that contradicts WHO's?

As Miltimore wrote, "Recent reports suggest US intelligence agencies relied heavily on WHO in its national assessment of the COVID-19 threat."

This is gravely concerning because bad information leads to bad policies. This is true not only for government policy (like mayors, governors, and heads of state deciding to largely shut down the economy in their jurisdiction), but for the policies of private decision-makers like doctors, business-owners, and individuals making decisions about the health and overall lives of themselves and their families.

Indeed, WHO's misinformation early in the crisis squandered the most precious part of the world's prep time, which likely crippled the public's responses and may have cost many lives.

YouTube risks compounding that tragedy by now insisting that the public's response to the coronavirus emergency conforms even more strictly with WHO's dubious pronouncements. Wojcicki wants to protect WHO's recommendations from contradiction. But WHO's recommendations are necessarily informed by WHO's information, which has proven to be extremely suspect. Sheltering untrustworthy pronouncements risks amplifying their dangerous influence.

Why Censorship Is Counter-Productive

So, it is ironic that YouTube justifies this policy in the name of protecting the public from dangerous misinformation.

It is true that many videos contradicting official pronouncements are themselves full of medical quackery and other misleading falsehoods. But, censorship is the worst way to combat them.

For one, censorship can actually boost the perceived credibility of an untruth. Believers interpret it as validation: evidence that they are onto a truth that is feared by the powers-that-be. And they use that interpretation as a powerful selling point in their underground evangelism.

Censorship also insulates falsehoods from debunking, allowing them to circulate largely uncriticized in the dark corners of public discourse.

This makes censorship especially counterproductive because it is open-air debunking that is one of the most effective ways to counter misinformation and bad ideas. As Justice Louis Brandeis expressed in a US Supreme Court opinion, the ideal remedy for bad speech, "is more speech, not enforced silence."

Again, YouTube has a right to set the terms of service of its own website. But the general principle applies here as well: the truth has a much better fighting chance with a proliferation of competing voices than with inquisitorial efforts to circumscribe discourse within a narrow orthodoxy.

A Systematic Problem

Moreover, WHO's track record of misinformation is not exceptional among government organizations in neither its degree of error nor in its disastrous impact. Governments and the experts they employ not only get things wrong but have frequently proven to be fundamentally wrong-headed on big questions.

To take another example in the realm of public health, it is increasingly widely recognized that the high-carb, low-fat diet recommendations, as depicted by the the USDA's "Food Pyramid," and successfully promoted for decades to the population by the US government and the most respected authorities on dietary science and epidemiology, was basically backward. Science journalist Gary Taub tells the whole story of bad science, corrupt influence, and obtuse orthodoxy in his book *Good Calories, Bad Calories*.

Again, bad information leads to bad advice, which leads to bad choices. So how much illness and even death was caused by generations of Americans uncritically swallowing "official" diet advice and by Americans largely only having one choice on the "menu" of diet advice?

The more we centralize decision-making and the management of actionable information, the wider the scope of the damage caused by any single error. But if we let a thousand errors bloom along with a thousand truths, any single error will be circumscribed in its damage and more likely to be corrected through experience and counter-argument.

Knowledge Problems

Champions of policies like YouTube's like to cast the issue in simplistic terms: as a black-and-white battle between respectable experts and wild-eyed crackpots. But the issue is more complex than that.

It is just as often a matter of overweening technocrats making pronouncements on matters that are way beyond them in complexity, that involve factors that fall way outside their domain of expertise, and that drastically impact the lives of millions or even billions. For example: a few dozen epidemiologists, with limited understanding of economics and a great many other relevant disciplines, holding sway over whole economies.

It is also a matter of *dissenting* experts being silenced along with the actual crackpots.

And, perhaps most fundamentally, it is a matter of weakening the individual's ability to discern between truth and falsehood, good advice and bad, by denying them the responsibility and practice of doing so in the first place—of turning self-reliant, free men and women into irresponsible wards to be led by the nose like dumb, deferential livestock by their "expert" caretakers.

That is not where we are, but that is the direction that the rigid enforcement of centralized orthodoxies tends toward.

A Challenge

Let's choose a different direction. YouTube, do better. Trust your users more. Treat them like human beings with all the capacities for learning, growth, discourse, and cooperation that are the distinctive glories of being human.

After all, that is what made you great in the first place. Your very name is derived from your original faith in the individual. YouTube (a crowd-sourced, individual-driven, pluralistic platform) is what made the boob tube (centralized, institutionalized, and homogenizing broadcast television) largely obsolete. As such, you had a starring role in the internet's democratization of information and learning.

Don't betray that legacy. Not now. Not when we need open platforms for the free flow of information and discourse more than ever.

Current Controversies

Chapter 3

Is Media Bias Degrading Media Trustworthiness?

Overview: TV News Outlets Overrepresent Extreme Partisanship

Denise-Marie Ordway

Denise-Marie Ordway is an award-winning journalist. She joined the Journalist's Resource in 2015 after working as a reporter for newspapers and radio stations in the US and Central America, including the Orlando Sentinel *and* Philadelphia Inquirer. *Her work also has appeared in publications such as* USA Today, *the* New York Times, *the* Chicago Tribune, *and the* Washington Post.

Major network and cable TV news outlets have given the most airtime to members of Congress with the most extreme views, creating a perception there is greater division among elected leaders than actually exists, researchers have found.

Their analysis indicates broadcast news outlets—Americans' primary source for political news—are partly to blame for growing political polarization in the U.S. and voters' heightened dislike for members of the opposing political party.

"The Congress that gets reported in the media is a different ideological distribution than Congress as it exists," one of the study's authors, Joshua P. Darr, an assistant professor of political communication at Louisiana State University, tells Journalist's Resource. "The media feature these extreme legislators and that makes Congress seem more extreme than it is."

While extreme partisan politics have drawn significant TV news coverage since President Donald Trump's election in 2016, the problem pre-dates the Trump era by a decade or more.

The analysis that Darr and his colleagues conducted, published in the *Journal of Communication* in December 2019, focuses on

"Research: TV News Outlets Overrepresent Extreme Partisans in Congress (Plus: 4 Tips for Better Coverage)," by Denise-Marie Ordway, The Journalist's Resource, January 17, 2021. https://journalistsresource.org/media/research-tv-news-outlets-overrepresent-extreme-partisans-in-congress-plus-4-tips-for-better-coverage/.

members of the U.S. Houses of Representatives and their statements aired on news programs on ABC, CBS, NBC, CNN, Fox News and MSNBC. The researchers examined a combined 46,218 transcripts of national TV news programs broadcast between Jan. 3, 2005, and Jan. 3, 2013, representing the 109th through the 112th sessions of Congress.

"There were more televised statements by extreme members and fewer statements by moderate members across all networks and network types," the researchers conclude in their paper, "As Seen on TV? How Gatekeeping Makes the U.S. House Seem More Extreme." Darr's two co-authors are Jeremy Padgett, an assistant professor of communication at the University of Mobile in Alabama, and Johanna Dunaway, an associate professor of political science at Texas A&M University.

Darr says the most partisan lawmakers likely have sought and been given even more airtime in recent years, especially since Trump took office.

Republican legislators soon discovered that appearing on TV news programs was an easy way to communicate directly with the president, known to watch national news broadcasts and Fox News in particular, Darr explains.

"Media coverage on partisan networks, if anything, has gotten more important for members of Congress," Darr says.

The researchers point out in their paper that both Fox News, which leans right, and CNN, which tends to lean left, gave more airtime to Republicans with extreme views than Democrats with extreme views. They also write that left-leaning MSNBC "seems to have prioritized content from the most conservative members of the House … possibly in an effort to present negative exemplars to liberal audiences for criticism."

CBS, on the other hand, gave more airtime to far-right members of the House than to other conservative legislators. But the network gave the most airtime to far-left and left-leaning House members, according to the paper.

The Consequences of Covering Extreme Politics

Dunaway warns that TV news programs will continue incentivizing extreme politics if they do not stop giving the most attention to the most partisan lawmakers and focusing on party conflict. And that, she says, will result in an even deeper division among members of the two political parties.

"We know that the public often relies on signals from elites to help inform their impressions of the parties as well as to clarify the differences between them," Dunaway wrote to JR in an email. "As long as these outlets are depicting members as more uniformly extreme than they actually are, members of the public will have misperceptions about the degree to which elite partisans differ across policy issues and perhaps even the degree to which there is animosity between the two parties."

Another potential consequence: Fewer moderate politicians will seek office.

"Moderates are unlikely to run for Congress if they perceive a lack of fit with the national party," the researchers write in their paper. "The media's rewards for ideological extremity in Congress could prove self-reinforcing, by encouraging extreme voting behavior and discouraging moderates from running for office."

The Loss of Local News

Darr says the decline of local journalism nationwide has contributed to the problem. Local news outlets experiencing financial losses in recent years have cut staff and coverage while some smaller newspapers have shuttered completely.

Without local news coverage, members of Congress have less incentive to prioritize the needs and demands of people living in their legislative districts, Darr says. Historically, local newspapers and TV and radio stations often interviewed federal legislators for local stories, especially after a successful push for funding or new policies benefitting voters in their home states.

"If the media gatekeepers' tendency toward extremity and conflict are rewarding people who use conflict in their words and they're doing it at the national level, then that's what the legislators are going to pursue," Darr notes. Likewise, he adds, if newsrooms run stories looking at whether or not legislators are doing work that benefits their constituents, legislators will put more effort into helping their constituents.

Earlier research from Darr and Dunaway focusing on local newspapers found that in some parts of the country where newspapers had closed, voters became more polarized. They were more likely to vote along party lines in key races and less likely to choose candidates from multiple political parties.

A new book by Darr, Dunaway and Matthew Hitt, an associate professor of political science at Colorado State University, further examines how local newspapers affect political polarization in their communities.

The book, *Home Style Opinion: How Local News Can Slow Polarization*, is scheduled for release this spring. One of its main takeaways: Political polarization began to spread more slowly in one California city after a newspaper there stopped running opinion page pieces about national issues for a month in 2019.

Tips for Journalists

There are several things journalists can do to improve their coverage of Congress and prevent political polarization—or at least not make it worse, Darr and Dunaway explain. Here are their suggestions:

- Journalists should think carefully about which members of Congress they mention and quote in their news stories. "Just as they might strive to ensure that they select members who are representative in terms of race, ethnicity, geography, and gender, they should also be mindful of trying to represent the range of views on either side of the aisle (at least as long as there is still a range of views)," Dunaway told JR by email.
- Use Voteview, a project launched by two researchers at Carnegie-Mellon University, to gain a better understanding of federal legislators' voting patterns, ideological positions and party loyalty. The website provides ideology scores and

tracks how often a member of Congress agrees with their party's majority position on a vote.

- When reporting on members of Congress, include local context such as what the House member or U.S. senator has done for voters back home. National journalists should reach out to local reporters for insights, Darr says. "To the extent you can, talk about the local angle and not just partisan conflict," he recommends, adding that national TV news programs should feature local journalists to report out their stories. "Get a local reporter on TV. That could take the focus off partisan conflict and extremity and put it on what they [legislators] are doing for their constituents."
- Remind audiences that despite their differences, members of Congress have been able to work together successfully over the years. Even amid conflict, they have created and approved new policies and amended and adopted budgets. "Talking about division foments division," Darr says. "Spotlighting times when compromises were reached and bills were passed can be a useful complement to stories on partisan division."

Fox News Creator Roger Ailes Destroyed Objectivity

Neal Gabler and Bill Moyers

Neal Gabler is the author of five books and the recipient of two Los Angeles Times Book Prizes, Time *magazine's nonfiction book of the year,* USA Today*'s biography of the year, and other awards. He is also a senior fellow at the Norman Lear Center at the University of Southern California. Bill Moyers is an American journalist and political commentator. He served as the White House press secretary under the Johnson administration and was a director of the Council on Foreign Relations from 1967 to 1974.*

Fox News creator and former chief Roger Ailes, who died at 77 last week from complications after a fall in his Florida home, may have been the most significant political figure of the last 35 years—which isn't necessarily a compliment to those of us who believe media mavens shouldn't also be political operatives.

Ailes clearly thought differently. He simultaneously changed the contours both of American politics and American media by melding them, and in doing so changed the contours of fact and objectivity as they once were understood before the era of post-fact.

It seems a lot to put on one man, but Roger Ailes destroyed the idea of media objectivity in the name of media objectivity, the way a phony evangelist might destroy virtue in the name of virtue. Things have never been the same since.

Ailes was a political acolyte of Richard Nixon, and Nixon was a media acolyte of Ailes. It was a perfect and powerful alliance—two outcasts seeking retribution. Nixon's great contribution to American politics was to take his personal umbrage, a lifetime of slights, and nationalize it. Like so many among the aggrieved, he aspired to be an insider and was tormented by not being admitted to their ranks.

"Roger Ailes: The Man Who Destroyed Objectivity," by Neal Gabler and Bill Moyers—represented by Doctoroff Media Group, LLC, May 23, 2017. Reprinted by permission.

In anger, he took them on, especially those he regarded as haughty elites—accused spy Alger Hiss, who was the personification of the Ivy-educated aristocrat and on whose takedown Nixon built his career; John Kennedy, who was everything Nixon wanted to be and wasn't; and the entire liberal establishment, which would denigrate and denounce him as he rose through the political ranks. He became the avatar for every person who had suffered the same disdain and abuse, and he turned Republicanism into a therapeutic movement of social vengeance.

Ailes was no less an outcast. Born in small-town Ohio, a pudgy hemophiliac bedridden for months at a time, bullied and baited, he nursed grievances against the same folks as Nixon. When they met, while Nixon was making an appearance on *The Mike Douglas Show*, which Ailes produced, Ailes found his vehicle. Ailes converted his resentments and Nixon's into a media message, and just as Nixon was able to nationalize it politically, Ailes would eventually nationalize it media-wise, first by becoming Nixon's communications adviser, and then by bringing that experience to television news.

It was no accident that Nixon and Ailes not only shared grievances, but also constituencies. The base of conservatism—especially those angry old white men who had supported Nixon—would be the viewership of Fox News, too. These were people who felt the world slipping away from them in the tumult of civil rights, feminism, counter-culturalism and multiculturalism; people who abhorred change; people who felt the political system was stacked against them; and more. The vector of history was pointed in the wrong direction: forward. Politically, they blamed Democrats, who seemed sympathetic to change. Culturally, they would come to blame the media, which reported on this new narrative of a changing world without expressing disapproval of it.

Exploiting the latter was Ailes' job. He constructed a snarling counternarrative in the media in which social change was not a sign of progress but rather a sign of decadence and decay. If you boil Fox News down to one basic idea, this is it: White people are losing the world, the world is going to hell as a result, and liberal elites, including the liberal media, ought to pay.

Degrading the mainstream media wasn't easy, despite these willing, disgruntled viewers, readers and listeners. For one thing, before Fox News, most people actually trusted the media. (*CBS Evening News* anchor Walter Cronkite was famously called the most trusted man in America.) The mainstream media weren't perceived as politically biased, and though there was certainly partisanship in newspapers, many of which tilted left or right, broadcast TV news was anodyne. Having to appeal to large swaths of the public and terrified of alienating prospective viewers, TV journalists generally walked the line between left and right. They reported. They didn't editorialize. Or at least they didn't think they editorialized.

And that is where Ailes came in. In essence, he convinced his public that simple reporting was a form of editorializing. He suggested that the media's so-called "facts" about the changing world were an endorsement of that world, and he claimed to be exposing media bias in order to correct it. In a way, he took seriously Stephen Colbert's joke, "It is a well-known fact that reality has a liberal bias." But it could only happen because cable television, unlike broadcast television, could survive on a relatively small demographic niche like angry old white men. In Fox News, they found an outlet for their rage.

You could say that Fox News gave voice to those who felt voiceless, though it might be more accurate to say that he gave voice to those who were so filled with enmity that they seemed on the borderline of sanity. With his hosts and guests howling at elites without surcease, he created not just an alternative media or even an alternative set of facts, but an alternative universe that has overtaken the real one—a bizarre universe bubbling with resentments and conspiracies and fabrications in which liberals aren't a political opposition; they are the source of all evil. Basically, he poisoned America.

It was a brilliant strategy. Ailes not only turned those white men against broadcast television (and most of the other establishment media, about whom these folks weren't too happy to begin with); he turned them against the idea of objectivity itself. Or to put it plainly: News that wasn't biased toward the right couldn't possibly be objective.

"Fair and balanced" was the slogan with which he branded his ultra-conservative, mainstream-media bashing network—meaning, of course, that the mainstream media weren't fair to the right and were unbalanced to the left. What he, and even many of his critics, didn't acknowledge is that the words "fair and balanced" don't stand in consonance with one another but in contrast. To be balanced is not necessarily to be fair since fairness demands one go where the facts lead, whatever the direction, though neither fairness nor balance were really Ailes' causes. His cause was unfairness and unbalance—to disrupt the normal flow of fact and reportage and replace fact with right-wing opinion in order to get his vengeance against the left. He won there too.

(One of Ailes' cleverer tactics was a show called *Fox News Watch* in which he had media critics analyze news coverage. For five years I was one of them, a token liberal, and Ailes was smart enough to let me brutalize week after week the network on which I was appearing.)

Ailes was subtle in another way that may actually have had more impact in undoing objectivity than his conservative bloviating bludgeons like Bill O'Reilly and Sean Hannity. He understood that undoing objectivity wasn't just a function of skewing the news and blending it with commentary so that the two seemed inextricable; it was a function of revising the entire media environment. To that end, Ailes turned television news into tabloid news, undoing objectivity by doing what tabloid newspapers had always done: undoing seriousness.

Ailes got his start in entertainment, and he brought those talents to his network, blending news not just with noise but with showbiz. Fox News became anti-news. Most news outlets opted for a studied monochronism. Fox News was loud and colorful. Most sought to unclutter their broadcasts. Ailes sought to crowd them with the zipper across the bottom of the screen and screaming graphics. Most sought to emphasize reportorial authority. Ailes emphasized verbal muscle-flexing among the male hosts and sexiness among the women. Long before Ailes was accused of sexual harassment, the network's attitude toward women was there for everyone to see—or ogle. The leering sexuality he brought to Fox News wasn't incidental to its success; it was instrumental to it, both in the sexual politics it purveyed and in the smarminess it conveyed. The message was: This isn't real news because there is no real news. Real news is just a media pretense.

Ailes' network, then, was a wild journalistic carnival designed to turn everything upside down and hit the media where it was most vulnerable: its own sense of seriousness. Fox News was a world of anger, accusation, cynicism, excitement, sex, heat and oversold headlines. Everything but gravitas.

If this sounds more than vaguely familiar, it is because the measure of how powerfully Fox News has penetrated the American consciousness is the presidency of Donald Trump. Trump is fully the creation of Fox News, the candidate of Ailes' dreams, the man who came to embody the two most important aspects of Fox News—its betrayal of truth and its allegiance to journalistic porn. And this is why Ailes is so important in our political and media ecologies. We think of how Republicanism in the post-Reagan era infected the media, and we see Fox News as the prime example. But we don't think as much about how Fox News infected Republicanism. Ailes was the carrier, and Trump the result.

Without Fox News, the Republican Party might look different—and better. Without Fox News to conflate entertainment with news, to rip apart the idea of a serious media, to push a single-minded partisan agenda and to enflame embittered white men, there would have been no foundation on which Trump could build his candidacy—or for that matter, no platform from which to blast an unending stream of nonsense stories about Benghazi and emails and the Clinton Foundation that the mainstream media felt duty-bound to pick up. No political party had ever had a major national propaganda arm posing as a media outlet. Ailes gave the Republicans one, and took the soul of the party in return.

The damage that Roger Ailes did to the media, to our political discourse, and to objectivity is incalculable. The most significant man of his political generation, he may also have been the most dangerous. It is one hell of a legacy—and probably a lasting one.

People Don't Trust the News and Social Media

Ricardo Bilton

Ricardo Bilton is a contributor at the Nieman Journalism Lab. He was previously a reporter at Digiday, where he covered the business of digital media. He's also written for VentureBeat, ZDNet, the New York Observer, *and the* Japan Times.

A new report from the Reuters Institute for the Study of Journalism offers a bit more insight into what's driving distrust in news organizations across the world.

Working with YouGov, the Reuters Institute for the Study of Journalism polled around 18,000 people across nine countries (U.S., Germany, UK, Ireland, Spain, Denmark, Australia, France, and Greece) to gather qualitative data about people's trust in news and social media. After respondents were asked whether they agreed with statements like "the news media does a good job in helping me distinguish fact from fiction," they were invited to share their reasons in an open-ended text box. Reuters' Nic Newman and Richard Fletcher coded these 7,915 responses to categorize the issues and concerns that are fueling peoples' distrust.

Here's some of what they found:

Why Don't People Trust the News? Concern About Bias, Spin, and Hidden Agendas

Two-thirds of people (67 percent) cited one of these factors as a reason they don't trust what they read. Unsurprisingly, concerns about political biases were particularly significant in the U.S., where 34 percent of respondents who distrusted news media cited concerns about political bias as the reason why. This concern is even more acute among those on the political right, who were

"Why Don't People Trust the News and Social Media? A New Report Lets Them Explain in Their Own Words," by Ricardo Bilton, The President and Fellows of Harvard College, November 30, 2017. Reprinted by permission.

three times more likely to distrust the news media than those on the left. (Three responses featured in the report: "Liberal media is full of bulls*** and lies," "Fox News keeps it fair; CNN tells us left-wing lies," and "They are so far to the left, they might fall off.")

Trust Takes Time to Build but Can Quickly Evaporate

One telling finding from the report is that trust in news is significantly higher among people above the age of 35 (42 percent) than those younger than 35 (34 percent) and people of low income (35 percent). The authors suggest that this difference emerges because wealthier, older people are more likely to be invested in the status quo, but also because trust is a product of "stories turning out to be accurate and fair again and again," which takes time to recognize. Brands, particularly journalistic ones, don't gain trust overnight, and it may be a long while before news organizations see their renewed emphasis on fact-checking and journalistic transparency pay off among readers broadly.

Video Is a Key Driver of Trust

If you want people to trust what you say, show, don't tell. Because television is seen as less open to manipulation compared to text and photos, respondents said that the presence of visuals gives them more confidence that a news report is true. "Usually, the news media can offer images or video or interviews or statements that show what they are reporting or that they are from official sources," said one respondent in Australia.

Of course, it's a scarily likely possibility that even this could change as new technology makes it easier to fake video footage as well.

People Have a Complicated Relationship with Social Media

It's telling that, while social media has become a central source of news for many people, just 24 percent of respondents said that social media does a good job of helping them separate fact from fiction. Put another way, just because people are on Twitter and Facebook all day doesn't mean they trust everything (or even most things) that they read. This is true across age, gender, and income status. Roughly 35 percent of respondents who distrust social media cited the lack of fact-checking and the prevalence of opinion-driven information as the most significant reasons. (Notably, just five percent of these people said they lacked confidence in social media because of a distrust in virality and the platforms' algorithms, suggesting either that few are concerned about technology's role in presenting the news they read, or that few are aware of it.)

On the other hand, 33 percent of those that do trust what they read on social media point to the inherent benefits of the social platforms, which make it easier to encounter a range of voices that together can often give a fuller picture of a story and reveal gaps in knowledge.

"I can view multiple sources on the same issue or event, and there are people critiquing the articles and posts, so I can see where some things were skewed or reported narrowly," said one respondent in the U.S.

Fixing the Trust Problem Will Require Publishers, Platforms, and Readers to Work Together

While news organizations have taken pains to open up their reporting processes and provide readers with a variety of fact-checking services, Newman and Fletcher write that there is still a lot of work to do when it comes to distinguishing "their journalism better from the mass of information available on the internet." A shift away from digital advertising and toward more reader-supported business models could help news organizations focus less on click generation and more on deeper investigations that will help them build trust with readers. There's also a lot to be done with creating more representative media organizations that hire a more diverse range of people across age, economic outlook, race, and gender.

Facebook and Twitter, too, must grapple with their role in the trust problem, particularly when it comes to identifying trustworthy news sources on their platforms. (Facebook, for example, recently started to test a feature that would give news organizations a "breaking news" label for their stories.) Indeed, initiatives like The Trust Project and The News Integrity Initiative all involve input from both media and tech companies.

The authors conclude:

> Rebuilding trust will a long-term process and will require the commitment of publishers, platforms, and consumers over many years. Finding solutions requires a solid understanding of the perceptions and motivations of consumers, and this paper aims to contribute by providing at least a snapshot of current concerns. In many ways, we find audiences ahead of publishers and platforms in demanding change.

Trust in Local Media Is Higher Than in National Media

Damian Radcliffe

Damian Radcliffe is the Carolyn S. Chambers Professor in Journalism, a Professor of Practice, an affiliate of the Department for Middle East and North Africa Studies (MENA), and a research associate of the Center for Science Communication Research (SCR) at the University of Oregon.

With the polarization of America's media and politics reaching a fever pitch, many news consumers—"worn out by a fog of political news," as a recent *New York Times* feature put it—are responding by tuning out altogether.

Media distrust, which has intensified globally in recent years, is also a likely factor. A recent Gallup poll found only 13% of Americans trust the media "a great deal," while 28% indicated that they trust the media "a fair amount."

However, evidence suggests a more favorable situation for local journalism.

Poynter's 2018 Media Trust Survey and a recent Knight Foundation-Gallup study each found that trust in local media is higher than for national media.

Only 31% of Americans say they trust reporting from national news outlets "a great deal" or "quite a lot," while 45% of Americans say the same for reporting from local news organizations.

Forty-five percent still isn't great; clearly, there's work to be done. These efforts are complicated by the fact that many newsrooms are struggling financially.

Despite this backdrop, I'm optimistic. I've spent two decades researching and working in local news. I believe local media outlets

"Local News Outlets Can Fill the Media Trust Gap—But the Public Needs to Pony Up," by Damian Radcliffe, The Conversation, November 19, 2019. https://theconversation.com/local-news-outlets-can-fill-the-media-trust-gap-but-the-public-needs-to-pony-up-126637.

are in a position to creatively cater to audiences burned out by beltway drama.

Here are four ways local newsrooms can forge deeper relationships with the communities they serve.

1. Interact with Readers

With newsroom employment down 25% since 2008—the equivalent of 28,000 jobs—there are fewer boots on the ground. Nonetheless, opportunities to engage with audiences are greater than ever.

One way is to be visible—online and in real life.

Journalists can think about opportunities for face-to-face interaction with readers. Some outlets have started holding open editorial meetings, in which journalists discuss the stories they're developing, or meet-and-greets with the public. There are also opportunities to engage with readers via social media, whether it's through Facebook Live or Q&As on Reddit, also known as "Ask Me Anything."

These efforts matter, because local journalists are often the only journalists people ever meet. As a result, they can serve as a proxy for perceptions of the wider industry.

2. Teach the Process

Another way to build trust is to explain how journalism works.

Research suggests audiences don't understand how journalism is produced, nor do they understand some of the terminology reporters deploy.

For example, a 2018 survey found 60% of respondents believed reporters get paid by their sources "sometimes or very often." Joy Mayer, director of the Trusting News project, told me that when journalists talk about "anonymous sources," many people assume the journalist doesn't know who the source is, either.

It's not difficult to address this, and doing so could help engender more trust in journalistic practice.

In December 2018, for example, journalists at the *Oregonian* published a series about five seemingly disparate crimes and their connection to John Ackroyd, a convicted murderer. But they didn't just publish the pieces and wait for the awards. They also shared articles outlining their reporting methods, alongside an annotated version of the full series with footnotes and links to related documents.

3. Give Readers What They Want

Without this type of transparency, as a recent Knight report acknowledged, trust in local news "is vulnerable to the same perceptions of partisan bias that threaten confidence in the national media."

One further way to try to eliminate this is to cede some control to the audience.

In an article published by Harvard's Nieman Lab, newsroom consultant Jennifer Brandel and editor Mónica Guzmán argue that it's important for journalists to shift their approach to coverage.

The editorial meeting of the future, they write, "won't start with our ideas—we'll start with the information gaps the public demonstrates they have, and focus our efforts squarely on filling those gaps."

Getting audiences to submit questions and listening to their needs can actually result in stories that journalists might not otherwise have produced.

The Knight Foundation's recent research highlighted opportunities to put this principle into operation. Nearly two-thirds of their respondents want more coverage on subjects like drug addiction, K-12 education, the environment and planned public works. They also want local outlets to do a better job holding those in power accountable.

4. Encourage Readers to Pay

However, the uncertain finances of many small newsrooms are a major roadblock to experimentation and giving readers the content they crave.

Declining revenue has meant more than 1 in 5, or 1,800, local newspapers have closed since 2004. Today, over 1,300 communities lack original local reporting.

Most readers simply don't realize how dire the situation is for some outlets.

According to the Pew Research Center, 71% of Americans "think their local news media are doing just fine financially." This may explain why only 14% of them financially supported a local news source in the past year.

Yet readers indicated that they "were more likely to subscribe or otherwise support their local newspaper if it were the only one in their area and at risk of shutting down."

New research shows that audiences value local news, and 61% of Americans say their local news organizations do an "excellent" or "good" job covering what's going on in their area. But the Knight Foundation's latest report, "Putting a Price Tag on Local News," also finds that few readers are currently paying for it.

Clearly, many readers don't realize how precarious things are. Newsrooms therefore must make a better case for the value of their work and why it needs to be supported.

A Civic Imperative

Until then, local outlets will have to do more with less.

This isn't easy. But even the smallest newsrooms, like the *Cottage Grove Sentinel* in Oregon, have been able to successfully experiment with new formats and ways to engage with readers.

Americans believe local news outlets are accurate, useful, trustworthy and caring. Yet without a vibrant local news industry, fewer people run for office and citizens become less engaged about elections.

"The diminishment of local news is to democracies what climate change is to the environment," argues Tim Franklin, the head of Northwestern University's Medill Local News Initiative.

"It's a slow-motion crisis, the effects of which we're just beginning to see."

The appetite for hard-hitting, relevant, local news is clearly there. The big question is how best to tap into it and satiate it—all while ensuring local journalists can pay the bills.

Partisan Bias Has Existed for Most of Media's History

Matt Grossmann

Matt Grossmann is a senior fellow of the Niskanen Center and associate professor of political science and director of the Institute for Public Policy and Social Research at Michigan State University. He is a coauthor of Asymmetric Politics: Ideological Republicans and Interest-Group Democrats *(Oxford University Press, 2016) and the author of* Artists of the Possible: Governing Networks and American Policy Change Since 1945 *(Oxford University Press, 2014).*

In the age of Fox News Channel, talk radio, and MSNBC, it is tempting to think we have entered an unprecedented age of biased media. But partisan bias is actually the norm in media history. As Jonathan Ladd argues, "The existence of an independent, powerful, widely respected news media establishment is an historical anomaly. Prior to the twentieth century, such an institution had never existed in American history."

In the nineteenth century, overtly partisan newspapers were the norm. Independent journalism was a successful countervailing movement that brought with it standards of unbiased political coverage. Joseph Pulitzer, the Democratic politician and newspaperman, helped establish the Columbia School of Journalism in 1912 and the Pulitzer Prizes in 1917. The American Society of Newspaper Editors codified an impartiality principle in its 1923 code of ethics: "News reports should be free from opinion or bias of any kind."

But Republicans have long been skeptical of the ability of an independent press to equally represent their views. Donald Trump's declaration of any contrary coverage as "fake news" is a more extreme version of a long-standing complaint. As Ladd finds, "criticism of the institutional news media was a defining characteristic" of the conservative movement and Barry Goldwater's nomination campaign. His supporters later founded the Committee to Combat Bias in Broadcasting and Accuracy in Media to monitor the news for bias. Complaints about media bias were common in subsequent Republican administrations and eventually came to dominate Republican campaigns. One study found that 92% of claims of media bias in the 1988, 1992, and 1996 elections came from Republicans alleging liberal bias.

These complaints were directly tied to the rise of explicitly conservative media as alternatives to mainstream news. Kathleen Hall Jamieson and Joseph Capella, who studied the Rush Limbaugh show for a full year, found that he mentioned media bias every single day. Fox News Channel was created to counter perceived liberal bias, calling itself "fair and balanced" with the motto "we report, you decide."

Conservative skepticism of the ability of an independent press to be unbiased was a reaction to the basic demographics of journalism. Reporters have been and remain disproportionately Democrats and liberals (compared to the general public). Lars Willnat and David Weaver found that the proportion of Republican reporters dropped from an already-low 26% in 1971 to 7% in 2013. Republicans and conservatives are more common in local television news, but are rarely seen at national mainstream news outlets.

Are the Mainstream Media Biased in Favor of Democrats and Liberalism?

Even if reporters are disproportionately Democrats and liberals, they may be able to produce unbiased news by pursuing objective evidence or balanced coverage. Do they succeed?

Overall, studies examining the content of news coverage have not found consistent evidence of bias favoring Democrats or Republicans across many different elections. There are studies finding Republican bias and studies finding Democratic bias.

Others find only media bias toward the frontrunner, regardless of party. Dave D'Alessio examines 99 prior studies of presidential election coverage bias and finds no consistent partisan bias.

In an analysis of 95 Senate elections, Adam Schiffer finds that factors like incumbency, finances, poll standing, competitiveness, the state of the economy, and scandals explain the bulk of variation. But he does find a remaining slight advantage for Democrats in newspaper tone, even accounting for these factors.

Even where careful researchers do find bias, they tend not to find that it favors the same party all the time. Kim Fridkin Kahn and Patrick Kenney examined the positive or negative tone of each article and its coverage of issues and candidate traits and counted the number of criticisms of each candidate. They found that newspaper coverage favors incumbent candidates that the newspaper endorsed on its editorial page. But systematic studies of this kind depend on research choices that affect the results. If one candidate is quoted attacking another candidate, that shows up as a criticism, but it could reflect either an accurate portrayal of the opposing candidate's message or a choice by the reporter to emphasize the criticism. If a reporter mentions that one candidate has raised more money than another, it reflects both a reality about the race and a choice to mention fundraising over another indicator of support.

One might think that cataloging only the clearest instances of media bias is a solution to this problem, but media bias could be subtle. One study found, for example, that candidates endorsed by a newspaper get better-looking photographs in that newspaper.

The most famous study of media bias, by Tim Groseclose and Jeffrey Milyo, compared citations of interest groups and think tanks by media outlets with citations by members of Congress. They reasoned that an unbiased media outlet would cite material equally from sources favored by legislators in each party and from each ideological perspective. They found that most media outlets disproportionately cited sources favored by Democratic and more liberal members. Their measure of media bias allowed them to compare media outlets with members of Congress on the same ideological dimension.

But another study found that Groseclose and Milyo's methodology did not produce stable estimates over time. All outlets they studied appeared to be more moderate or conservative in later years. Brendan Nyhan leveled a different critique of Groseclose and Milyo: Democratic office holders and media organizations both cited more neutral experts, rather than favoring liberal perspectives: "Technocratic centrist to liberal organizations like Brookings and the Center on Budget and Policy Priorities tend to have more credentialed experts with peer-reviewed publications than their conservative counterparts." But conservatives also tend to doubt the ability of academic experts to maintain neutrality for the same reason that they are skeptical of the media: academics are also disproportionately Democrats and liberals. So the media bias debate reflects a broader conflict over whether technocratic expertise can be seen as neutral.

Despite these difficulties, studies of the relative treatment of Democratic and Republican candidates and their affiliated interest groups are relatively easy to conduct because there is a straightforward comparative baseline: balanced coverage of each candidate or each group. But that means the focus has been mostly on partisan biases, especially in election coverage, rather than broader ideological biases in the selection or description of political issues and events.

It may be easier, however, for reporters to treat two general election candidates or two parties in a congressional debate equally than it is to avoid ideological influences on coverage that stem from the reporters' underlying values. There is no evidence of a reporters' conspiracy to help the Democrats, but reporters with liberal viewpoints might (even inadvertently) choose different news to cover or frame it differently than does the much smaller number of conservative reporters.

The Promise of New Measures of Media Bias

State-of-the-art measures of media bias build on Groseclose and Milyo's strategy of comparing media outlets with members of Congress, but use "big data" approaches geared toward analyzing large sets of texts. This approach tries to capture more subtle biases in the use of language or the discussion of issues, which it might be more difficult for reporters to control.

In 2010, Matthew Gentzkow and Jesse Shapiro used the full 2005 Congressional Record to generate phrases disproportionately used by more liberal or conservative members of Congress and then compare the usage of those phrases across newspapers. This approach sidesteps some of the objections to Groseclose and Milyo's methodology by going beyond group citations, but it is still dependent on the idea that liberal and conservative legislators both use equivalently biased phrases and that, to be unbiased, reporters should tend to use them in roughly equal measure.

The approach still raises perennial difficulties in interpretation. The phrases disproportionately used by Democrats, according to Grentzkow and Shapiro, include some partisan messaging tropes—such as "workers' rights," "nuclear option," "sniper rifles," and "privatize Social Security"—but also nonpartisan, generic terms such as "trade agreement," "American people," "budget deficit" and "war in Iraq." Other Democratic phrases, such as "veterans' health care," "Congressional Black Caucus," and "minimum wage" reflect real partisan differences, but these are differences in issue agenda rather than message. Republican phrases similarly include poll-tested partisan language such as "death tax," "illegal aliens," "oil for food scandal," and "personal retirement accounts," but also neutral language referring to the names of courts and justices. Again, there are phrases that reflect issue priorities but not biased analysis, such as "stem cell" and "government spending." When reporters use these phrases, it may reflect anything from the neutral language in a paper's style guide to biased choices of what issues to cover to unfairly repeating one side's message more often. It is also difficult to distinguish between a reporter echoing liberal or conservative talking points and one side just being more "on message" in their communications with reporters.

Gregory Martin and Ali Yurukoglu recently used the same method to look for biased phrase usage on CNN, Fox News, and MSNBC in 2000, 2004, and 2008. They turned up significant but unsurprising Republican bias on Fox News and Democratic bias on MSNBC. Yet once again, the word lists found to be biased (based on congressional communications) alternatively instill confidence and raise questions. The most "Democratic" phrases included neutral language like "African American," "Republican leadership," and "Bush administration," along with more partisan phrases like "social justice" and "working families." The most "Republican" phrases included neutral phrases like "federal government" and "new refinery," alongside such ideologically tinged language as "death tax," "illegal aliens," and "limited government."

In a thoughtful appendix, the authors use several alternative measures to find similar trends. They analyze each year independently and all years together, they use different estimators of ideological position based on the same texts, and they produce an alternative measure: the time given to Democratic and Republican guests on each network. All measures produce the same basic contrast: Fox News is to the right of CNN and MSNBC and Fox News and MSNBC are getting more polarized over time. There is no reason to doubt these basic findings.

The improvement in measurement is quite welcome. But scholars should not lose sight of qualitative differences among media outlets. Regardless of word usage patterns, we should still categorically distinguish between CNN, which goes out of its way to find balanced panels of commentators even if it does not always succeed, and Fox and MSNBC. Similarly, we should be able to separate the journalism displayed on such Fox programs as *Special Report with Bret Baier* and *Fox News Sunday* from clearly biased programming such as the *Sean Hannity Show*. Even if the front page of a nonpartisan newspaper is subtly biased, this is qualitatively different from the bias openly displayed on the editorial page.

Losing sight of that difference downplays the change wrought by the rise of openly partisan and ideological media.

Clever Ways to Study Media Bias

Assuming that scholars can measure the relative ideological position of news organizations, it is still more difficult to locate the zero point of unbiased news. As Tim Groeling has pointed out, we do not know the population of real-world events that might neutrally be covered, so it is hard to tell if news judgment is biased or reflects neutrality. Does Trump receive negative coverage because the press hates him, or because he has produced a lot of detrimental news for himself?

Several recent studies of media bias use clever methods to get around these difficulties, but do not find consistent results. One study used an experiment where similar letters to the editor favoring each presidential candidate were sent to different newspapers. The researchers, perhaps surprisingly, found that newspapers were more likely to publish the letter against the candidate that it had endorsed, possibly as a way of balancing the opinion section. But the judgment of the editors may not correspond to the choices of that newspaper's reporters.

Another useful method is to compare coverage of similar events. One study showed that the same level of approval ratings for different presidents was covered differently by each network, reflecting partisan biases. Another study compared the coverage of similar economic statistics in different administrations, finding that the partisan editorial stance of the newspaper was associated with more positive coverage of the same unemployment rate for the endorsed presidents, but that other economic statistics had no partisan slant. A third study used instances where members of Congress switch political parties to look at changes in coverage for the same members in different parties. It found no significant party differences.

Another difficulty is that even biased coverage could reflect the media outlet's perception of its audience's views, rather than its own biases. One useful study found biased newspaper coverage of unemployment based on the party holding the White House, but found that this bias was substantially moderated after a competing newspaper closed. Apparently the newspapers took partisan approaches primarily to distinguish themselves from the other paper in town.

Perceptions of Bias Are Reducing Trust in News and Empowering Partisan Media

Regardless of the academic research, the public, and political professionals, are responding to their own perceptions of bias. William Eveland and Dhavan Shah found that even when Republicans and Democrats watch the same coverage, Democrats believe that it is more favorable for the Republican candidates and vice versa. Another study found that even presenting the same information but varying the label of where it came from (CNN or Fox) also changes the perceptions of bias.

Not surprisingly, then, faith in the news media has been in decline across the board. Yet mainstream media outlets get especially poor trust ratings from conservatives. Because Republicans regularly cite political bias in the mainstream media, their electorate only trusts explicitly conservative alternatives.

Given the strength of partisanship in contemporary political life, it is understandable that Republicans would be more likely to suspect and react to perceived biases among (disproportionately liberal) reporters. It would be surprising if the political views of reporters did not in any way affect their selection of news stories or their portrayal of events.

Only two out of the hundred largest newspapers endorsed Trump in 2016, so there is no reason to believe that perceptions of bias will be diminishing any time soon. Trump's constant attacks on the media and invocations of "fake news" mean that the Republican electorate is likely to further reduce its trust in mainstream media and rely even more on explicitly conservative media. Fox News and talk radio have large effects on their audiences, and even on the friends of viewers and listeners who do not themselves watch or listen. They have also changed the behavior of legislators, instilling fears of primary challenges and base backlashes.

Even if Republican skepticism of mainstream media impartiality is justified, the rise of explicitly ideological media as the central information sources for Republicans is still alarming. It is as if Republicans reacted to perceived biases on the front page of the *New York Times* by deciding to only read the editorial page of the *Wall Street Journal*.

The die may therefore be cast for increasingly replacing traditional journalism with partisan media. Even as Democrats are more accepting of the mainstream news media, the recent doubling of MSNBC viewership suggests that liberals may eventually succeed at copying the conservative media model. The dominance of independent, trusted, putatively impartial media is not a natural state of affairs. It is a twentieth-century phenomenon that is not guaranteed to survive.

Be careful what you call biased news; complaints about mainstream journalism are empowering outlets that are not even trying to be even-handed.

Current Controversies

Chapter 4

Can Anything Be Done to Establish More Trust in the Traditional News Media?

Overview: Americans Believe Public Trust in the News Media Can Improve

Jeffrey Gottfried, Mason Walker, and Amy Mitchell

Jeffrey Gottfried is a senior researcher at the Pew Research Center, where he focuses on US public opinion about journalism and the news media. Mason Walker is a research analyst focusing on journalism and media. Amy Mitchell is director of journalism research at the Pew Research Center. She is responsible for the center's research related to news and information, including how the public accesses, engages with, and creates news, what news organizations are providing, and how technology is changing all of these elements.

In a year filled with major news stories—from impeachment to a contentious election, from a global pandemic to nationwide protests over racial injustice—Americans continue to have a complicated relationship with the news media.

While large swaths of the public often express negative views toward journalists and news organizations, a major Pew Research Center analysis—culminating a yearlong study on Americans' views of the news media—also finds areas where U.S. adults feel more affinity toward the media and express open-mindedness about the possibility that their trust in the industry could improve.

Many Americans remain skeptical toward the news media, questioning not only the quality of journalists' work but their intentions behind it. For instance, no more than half of U.S. adults have confidence in journalists to act in the best interests of the public, or think that other Americans have confidence in the institution. And the public is more likely than not to say to say that news organizations do not care about the people they report on.

"Americans See Skepticism of News Media as Healthy, Say Public Trust in the Institution Can Improve," by Jeffrey Gottfried, Mason Walker, and Amy Mitchell, Pew Research Center, August 31, 2020. Reprinted by permission.

While most Americans (61%) expect the news they get to be accurate, nearly seven-in-ten (69%) think news organizations generally try to cover up mistakes when they do happen.

The reasons for why Americans think these mistakes happen underscore the distrust that substantial portions of the public feel: Many say that careless reporting (55%) or even a desire to mislead the public (44%) are major factors behind significant mistakes in news stories, although other, less negligent or nefarious reasons such as the rapid pace of breaking news (53%) also are seen as responsible for mistakes.

Americans take issue with what they perceive as a lack of transparency by news organizations—both with respect to the work they do and the inner workings of their companies. Indeed, not only do many people see news outlets as opaque in how they produce their stories and choose their sources, but a large majority—72%—say news organizations do an insufficient job explaining to the public where their money comes from.

Six-in-ten U.S. adults also say news organizations are not forthcoming about conflicts of interest. On top of that, a vast majority of Americans (80%) think that the news they get is at least "somewhat" influenced by financial and corporate interests.

But findings from the study also suggest that the relationship between Americans and the media is not a lost cause. For one, the public gives the media fairly high marks for coverage of specific issues and events, including the recent coronavirus outbreak and the protests in the wake of the police killing of George Floyd.

And public skepticism toward the media does not appear to be purely antagonistic: Most Americans view some level of wariness toward the news media as healthy for a well-functioning society. Overall, 63% of U.S. adults say that, in an ideal world, it is better for society if Americans are skeptical of the news media. Far fewer (36%) say it is better if people are trusting of the news media.

Still, when asked directly whether Americans think their level of confidence in journalists can improve, three-quarters say such an outcome is possible.

This raises the question: Where might there be opportunities for the news media to gain more trust? First and foremost, the survey finds that personal connections with news tie strongly to Americans' views of the media overall, echoing earlier Pew Research Center findings at the local level. Americans who feel connected to news outlets—whether in feeling valued by, understood by or loyal to them—express far more positive views toward the news media. For instance, those who feel that their news sources value them are much more likely to expect their news to be accurate and to think news outlets are transparent with audiences.

According to the findings, there is plenty of room for improvement in this area: While most Americans want to have personal connections with their news sources, many do not experience it (again in line with previous Center findings on local news). More than half of U.S. adults say their news outlets do not particularly value them (57%) or that news organizations do not understand people like them (59%), and nearly two-thirds (63%) say they do not feel particularly loyal to the outlets they get their news from.

Americans' personal connections with specific news stories also are linked with their attitudes toward the media. When Americans encounter news stories that hit close to home, they generally have good things to say about the media's coverage. Roughly two-thirds of those who felt personally connected to a story—either because it covered an issue they believe they are an expert on, or because it was about a significant event that they experienced or witnessed—think that story was covered well. And those who feel this way express far more favorable views toward the news media in general than those who think the story was not covered well.

One of the most fundamental ways this manifests itself is in whether people think the news they get is accurate. About three-quarters of those who think that an issue in their wheelhouse or an event they experienced was covered well (74%) also believe the news they get overall is largely accurate. Among those who say that a story close to them missed the mark, just 39% expect to encounter accurate news; this group also is far more likely to feel that news organizations do not understand people like them.

Being transparent about corrections is another area where the public says news organizations have an opportunity to gain trust. While Americans perceive a range of reasons why mistakes in stories happen, about half (51%) say that seeing official corrections from news outlets makes them more confident in that outlet, compared with just 12% who say it makes them less confident.

These are among the key findings from a yearlong study of Americans' trust and attitudes toward the news media. This report draws on data included in a previously published report that looked at more than 50 Pew Research Center surveys; new survey data collected both before and during the COVID-19 outbreak; and a series of 10 focus groups conducted in three U.S. cities in November 2019. But the bulk of this report is based on previously unreleased data from a survey conducted Feb. 18-March 2, 2020, among 10,300 U.S. adults who are part of the Center's American Trends Panel. Quotations drawn from the focus groups are scattered throughout the report; these quotes are not intended to be representative of Americans' views. Instead, the quotations serve as examples of how everyday people think about these topics when they have the opportunity to express themselves in their own words.

Deep Partisan Divides in Views of the News Media, with Republicans Who Support Trump Most Critical

The first phase of this yearlong study established that partisanship is the strongest factor in Americans' views of the news media. And support for Donald Trump, who continues to strike a combative tone toward journalists, is another dividing line—particularly within the Republican Party.

One area in which this plays out is in perceptions of why errors occur in news stories. Republicans overall are more likely to think that mistakes happen because of ill will. Six-in-ten Republicans and

Republican-leaning independents cite a desire to mislead audiences as a major reason why significant mistakes make their way into news stories, compared with about a third of Democrats (32%) who feel this way. And within the GOP, this view is especially prevalent among Republicans who strongly approve of the job that Trump is doing as president.

But just because Republicans consistently express far more negative sentiments toward the news media does not mean that Democrats are always singing the media's praises. For example, Democrats—like Republicans—are more likely to say that news outlets do not care about the people they report on than say they do care.

There also are places where the two parties see more eye to eye. Majorities of both parties think it is beneficial for society to be skeptical of the news media, large portions think that confidence in the institution can increase, and they generally agree on the qualities that are important in choosing news sources.

Black Americans Seek Out News Sources That Cover People Like Themselves

The study also finds that beyond partisanship, there also are sharp differences across certain segments of the population in their attitudes of, relationships with and priorities for the news media. At a time when questions about representation in newsrooms are amplified in the wake of the protests in response to the killing of George Floyd, Black adults also are far more likely than others to say it is important to see themselves both in news coverage and in the newsroom.

When asked whether six different aspects of personal connections between news organizations and their audiences are important in deciding where to get their news from, Black Americans are more likely than White Americans to say each is at least somewhat important. But two factors related to representation stand out: Nearly seven-in-ten Black adults (68%) say it is at least somewhat important that their news outlets cover people like them, 27 percentage points higher than White adults (41%) and 14 points above Hispanic adults (54%). And nearly four-in-ten Black Americans (38%), along with a third of Hispanic Americans (33%), think it is important for the journalists themselves at a news outlet to look or sound like them, compared with just 13% of White Americans who say the same.

Focus on Truth, Not Fault

Jane E. Kirtley

Jane E. Kirtley is the Silha Professor of Media Ethics and Law at the Hubbard School of Journalism and Mass Communication at the University of Minnesota. She is also director of the Silha Center for the Study of Media Ethics and Law and is an affiliated faculty member at the University of Minnesota Law School.

After the fall of the Berlin Wall and the collapse of the Soviet Union, emerging democracies in Eastern and Central Europe began revising their constitutions and statutory laws to guarantee the rights of a free press. As part of that effort, in 1993, I traveled to Bucharest, Romania, to speak at a conference for nongovernmental organizations and other civil society groups. During one of the presentations, a trade union representative stood up and asked, "How do we make the press tell the truth?"

It struck me then that the question was naïve, if understandable. If you had lived in a society where all media were controlled by the Ceaușescu dictatorship and published only authorized propaganda, much of it false, it made sense to think that the opposite should prevail in the newly independent Romania. A free press should tell the truth. But as Pontius Pilate asked, "What is truth?" Who decides what is true? And who should compel the press to "tell the truth"?

"Fake News": Trump Didn't Invent the Term

There were no easy answers to these questions then, and 25 years later, we confront them again, not only in Europe, but in the United States and around the world. Politicians and their supporters accuse those in the mainstream media of peddling "fake news," a term

President Donald Trump claimed, in an October 2017 interview with Trinity Broadcasting Network, he invented.

In fact, he didn't. Perhaps the most notorious use of the equivalent term, "Lügenpresse" or "lying press," was invoked by the Nazis in the 1930s and revived by far-right anti-immigration activists in Germany in 2014 and by Trump supporters during the 2016 campaign to undermine public confidence in the mainstream media. But other groups across the political spectrum have used the term as well. As one example, the left-leaning Center for Democracy & Technology's PR Watch has been "reporting on spin and disinformation since 1993" with its "Stop Fake News!" campaign.

So, no, Trump didn't invent what he called "one of the greatest of all terms I've come up with." But he has been one of the prolific users of it. During his candidacy and since his election, he has applied the label of fake news to virtually any media—the "failing" *New York Times*, NBC, ABC, CBS, CNN, among others—he disagrees with or doesn't like. But he isn't alone. A poll conducted by Monmouth University reported that three out of four Americans believe that the media routinely report fake news, while a Gallup/Knight Foundation study found that 42 percent of Republicans consider any news stories that cast a political group or politician in a negative light to be fake news. The phrase has become so ubiquitous that *Washington Post* columnist Margaret Sullivan has argued that it should be discarded because its original meaning—"fabricated stories intended to fool you"—has been distorted beyond recognition.

Yet, the fake news label persists. Trump's inaugural "Fake News Awards," published on the Republican National Committee's website in January 2018, included several cases where news outlets had corrected themselves and apologized, actions that would not fit the traditional definition of fake news. In April 2018, more than 170 television stations owned by conservative-leaning Sinclair Broadcast Group were ordered to use local anchors to produce a scripted "must-run" commentary decrying fake news. Responding to criticism from others in the industry that the segment was itself fake news intended to deceive viewers, Trump tweeted that "the Fake News Networks, those that knowingly have a sick and biased AGENDA, are worried about the competition and quality of Sinclair Broadcast."

In June 2018, at the height of the controversy over the separation of undocumented immigrant families at the southern border, *Time* magazine's "Welcome to America" cover, juxtaposing a photograph of a crying Honduran toddler with one of a menacing Donald Trump on a red backdrop, was promptly labeled fake news because the child had not, in fact, been taken from her mother by federal agents. Defenders of the magazine claimed the cover was meant not as literal fact, but rather as a metaphor for the national debate. But for those looking for more evidence of fake news, *Time*'s cover provided it.

Weaponizing the "Fake News" Label

Despite Trump's incendiary tweets calling "the FAKE NEWS media" "the enemy of the American People," his actual power to take action to curtail their activities has, to date, been limited to largely unsuccessful attempts to exclude credentialed reporters from press briefings. But as Joel Simon of the Committee to Protect Journalists (CPJ) observed, in countries with less robust protections than the First Amendment, Trump's words provide authoritarian leaders in countries such as Kenya, Venezuela, and the Philippines the ammunition to suppress opposition media, even as they spread fake video clips and stories through paid commentators and bots. CPJ also reported that out of 262 journalists jailed around the world in 2017, 21 were arrested on "false news" charges. In April 2018, Malaysia, citing national security concerns, enacted the Anti-Fake News Act, which provides that anyone convicted of creating or circulating fake news online or in social media could face imprisonment for up to six years or fines in excess of $120,000.

Even mature democracies struggle with the issue of fake news. On January 1, 2018, Germany announced that it would begin to enforce a law, known as NetzDG, requiring social media sites to remove hate speech and fake news within 24 hours or face fines of up to 50 million Euros. In March 2018, the European Commission's High Level Group on fake news and online disinformation issued a report concluding that although disinformation may not necessarily be illegal, it nevertheless is harmful to democratic values. Although ostensibly eschewing "any form of censorship, either public or private," it advocates greater self-regulation in the short term, with a long-range goal of developing a Code of Practices to encourage transparency, media literacy, diversity, the development of tools to "tackle" disinformation, and further research to monitor and assess the sources and impact of fake news. On the other hand, also in March, the Dutch Parliament voted to repudiate EUvsDisinfo.eu, a European Union website created by the East Stratcom Task Force in 2015 to report disinformation and fake news allegedly spread by Russian actors. Its Dutch opponents characterize it as a state publication that "passes judgments whether a publication in the free media contains the correct views or not. If your publication ends up in its database, you're officially labeled by the EU as a publisher or disinformation and fake news."

These examples illustrate how problematic it can be when governmental entities become arbiters of what is true and what is fake. As the Dutch critics argued, governments should be loath to interfere in freedom of the press because "it makes it impossible for the truth to emerge in the public debate." This thinking was at the core of the seminal 1964 U.S. Supreme Court decision, *New York Times v. Sullivan.*

Constitutionalizing the Right to Be Wrong

The *Sullivan* case arose during the civil rights movement, involving a Montgomery, Alabama, public safety commissioner named L.B. Sullivan, who sued the *New York Times* after it published a fundraising advertorial that described law enforcement actions designed to discourage protests by activists such as Martin Luther King Jr. and his followers. Sullivan claimed that the ad, which made several factually inaccurate allegations about the Montgomery police, had defamed him personally, even though he was not identified by name or title.

In other words, Sullivan claimed the publication was fake news. He sought and won $500,000 in damages, without being required under Alabama law to prove that his reputation was actually harmed. But in a decision by Justice William Brennan, the high court reversed, concluding that under the First and Fourteenth Amendments, public officials like Sullivan could prevail in a libel suit only if they were also able to show not only falsity, but actual malice on the part of the publisher. This term of art is defined as knowledge that the statement was false, or proof that the publisher acted with reckless disregard for the truth. A showing of hatred or ill will, known as common law malice, is not sufficient to meet that test.

According to Justice Brennan, because some factual errors are inevitable even in the most careful news reporting, this protection is essential to avoid media self-censorship, to promote vigorous reporting on government and public officials, and to preserve our "profound national commitment to the principle that debate on public issues should be uninhibited, robust and wide-open."

In subsequent years, the First Amendment protection expanded to include lawsuits by public figures as well as government officials. Alleging falsity was not enough. No doubt this situation is what prompted Donald Trump, first as a candidate and then as president, to float the idea that the law should be changed.

"Open Up the Libel Laws"

At a rally in Fort Worth, Texas, in February 2016, Trump vowed, "I'm going to open up our libel laws so when they write purposely negative and horrible and false articles, we can sue them and win lots of money. We're going to open up libel laws, and we're going to have people sue you like you've never got[ten] sued before." In March 2017, he claimed in a tweet that "The failing @nytimes has disgraced the media world. Gotten me wrong for two solid years. Change libel laws?" And in October, he complained that it is "frankly disgusting the press is able to write whatever it wants to write." He raised the issue again in January 2018, contending that "our current libel laws are a sham and a disgrace and do not represent American values."

Many would argue that existing libel laws are quintessentially American. Their sweeping protection of good faith errors, even when they harm a reputation, exceeds that of every other common law country, including Canada and the United Kingdom. This is why, in 2010, Congress passed the SPEECH Act, making foreign libel judgments unenforceable in the United States unless the legal standards in the other country offer at least as much protection to the defendant as the First Amendment. The statute was enacted to curtail libel tourism, where foreign nationals sue U.S. defendants in other nations' courts where the standards of proof are less demanding.

Perhaps these less demanding standards might be precisely what Trump seeks to establish. In a meeting with the *Washington Post*'s editorial board in March 2016, Trump, after complaining about the "enormous" and "incredible hatred" demonstrated by the media, was asked what new standard he would propose, and he replied, "I want to make it more fair from the side where I am, because things are said about me that are so egregious and so wrong, and right now according to the libel laws I can do almost nothing about it."

As frustrating as that might be for Trump, it is exactly Justice Brennan's point. As a commentator in *The Federalist* observed, freedom of the press is "too important to allow public figures . . . to use the courts to silence the publications of things they didn't like or that made them look bad." This brings us to the heart of the matter: Is Trump really bothered by falsehoods or by truthful reports that make him "look bad"? Libel law in the United States is, as then-10th Circuit Judge Neil Gorsuch wrote in *Bustos v. A&E Television Networks*, "not about compensating for damage done to a false reputation by the publication of hidden facts. It's about protecting a good reputation honestly earned." Libel suits are intended to provide compensation to those whose reputations have been harmed as a result of false statements made with actual malice. By design, that is a very difficult standard to meet.

Focus on Truth, Not Fault

Trump's musings remind me of proposals to reform libel law considered in the late 1980s and early 1990s. Driven by concerns about escalating punitive damages awards, and inspired by a 1987 study by University of Iowa professors concluding that most libel plaintiffs sue to vindicate their reputations, not for the money—a sentiment Trump echoed at his 2016 Texas rally, where he claimed "I'm not taking their [the media defendants'] money"—several prominent scholars, judges, and free press advocates argued for new approaches to libel law that would focus on truth or falsity, not fault.

In 1988, in a *Harvard Law Review* article, Judge Pierre N. Leval, then of the Southern District of New York, advocated creation of what he called the "no-money, no-fault" libel suit. Under Leval's system, plaintiffs could sue to obtain a declaratory judgment of falsity. The fault requirements of *Sullivan* and its progeny would not apply, because, Leval claimed, "the sole purpose" of the *Sullivan* standard was to protect the press from crippling monetary awards. He also argued that these "no-money, no-fault" trials would be simpler, more efficient, less expensive, and would protect the media from inquiries into their news-gathering practices. They would provide plaintiffs with a far greater chance of vindicating their reputations, which is really what most of them want, he wrote.

Also in 1988, the Libel Reform Project at Northwestern University issued "the Annenberg Proposal." Under the Annenberg model, a libel "victim" would have to request a retraction or opportunity to reply within 30 days of publication. If the defendant complied, any further legal action would be barred. If not, either the plaintiff or the defendant could compel any libel suit to be converted into a "no-fault, no-damages" declaratory judgment proceeding, where the only issue would be truth or falsity. A traditional suit for actual damages would remain an option, but only if the defendant agreed to it.

Neither of these proposals was adopted at the state level. However, in 1993, the Uniform Law Commission promulgated the Uniform Correction or Clarification of Defamation Act (UCCDA) making a correction/clarification request a prerequisite to a libel suit. Under the Uniform Act, if, after a correction or clarification was published, the case still went to trial, a prevailing plaintiff could recover only economic losses, not punitive damages. As of 2018, only North Dakota, Texas, and Washington had adopted the UCCDA.

Libel Reform Redux

Of course, President Trump cannot unilaterally "open up the libel laws" by executive fiat. Libel law consists of state, not federal, statutes, or judge-made constitutional or common law. But assuming Trump could persuade some state legislatures to adopt a version of the Annenberg or Leval proposals, would he be satisfied with a retraction or a declaratory judgment of falsity? Would he fit the Iowa study profile of the libel plaintiff who is seeking only vindication, not money?

I'm skeptical. Most media organizations have, of their own volition, corrected their mistakes in their coverage of Trump and his administration, such as when *Time*'s White House correspondent erroneously reported in January 2017 that the bust of Martin Luther King Jr. had been removed from the Oval Office. Yet, despite rapid and repeated digital corrections, Trump nevertheless condemned the story as "deliberately false reporting," including it in the "Fake News Awards" list published in 2018. He didn't seem appeased by corrections or apologies.

Perhaps Trump would prefer some version of the "no-money, no-fault" trial. Although proof of actual malice would be off the table in a "truth trial," the reality is that even then, "[i]t is the reporter's accuracy, integrity, professional reputation and standing that are ultimately at stake," as litigator Don Reuben argued in the *ABA Journal* in April 1989. He contended that the Annenberg proposal would "chill the hell out of the working press, the reporter and editor" by making it easier for plaintiffs to prevail in court. He feared that corporate media would be tempted to embrace the "no-fault, no damages" option, abandoning First Amendment defenses and sacrificing the reporter in the name of expediency. If that was true in 1989, it is even truer in 2018, when economic constraints encourage news organizations to reduce their financial exposure as much as possible. With its potential humiliation of the news organization and journalists as a bonus, the "no-money, no-fault" trial might be an option that Trump would relish.

All this begs the question of whether courts are the best entities to determine the official version of "the truth." Supporters of the Leval or Annenberg proposals asserted that the government has a legitimate interest in the accuracy, or inaccuracy, of media reports. This view is shared by many government officials and institutions around the world. Numerous studies posit that fake news affected voter choices in the 2016 election, in the Brexit referendum, and other political campaigns, posing a fundamental threat to democratic institutions. Logically, governments would have a duty to protect audiences from fake news. Yet, both the executive and legislative branches might be perceived as self-interested if they tried to evaluate truth or falsity. The courts may be the best alternative.

But they would be the best of a bad lot. However independent they may be, courts are still instrumentalities of the government. As First Amendment scholar Zechariah Chafee wrote, "We must always be careful not to assume that the findings of a tribunal on a controversial issue are THE TRUTH." The marketplace of ideas is imperfect but essential to facilitate the search for truth. Government can control and manipulate the flow of information about itself and its actors, so any determination of truth or falsity that fails to recognize the fundamental and coextensive right of the citizen to criticize without fear of sanctions or retribution—

what Justice Brennan called "the central meaning of the First Amendment"—is flawed. A free and independent press, not a single leader or a government-run "Truth Tribunal," is the best means to ensure an informed citizenry, and to hold institutions and individuals to account. And that's not fake news.

How to Spot Real and Fake News

Emerald Works Limited

Emerald Works is a leading digital first provider of workplace performance support tools and resources. It pursues its vision through the internationally recognized and respected product and service brand Mind Tools, trusted, on-demand resources that help ambitious people to perform, manage, and lead with confidence.

When Alice scrolls through her social media feed, she's stopped in her tracks by the news that her company is about to be bought out by its biggest rival. She quickly posts a response, shares the story with her contacts, and emails it to her team so that they can discuss it later.

But then Alice has a troubling thought. What if the story wasn't true? What if she just shared a "fake news" story? After all, she didn't check the source.

If she has been a victim of fake news, and then added to the rumor mill herself, how will people ever trust her again?

Fortunately, there's lots you can do to avoid making the same mistake as Alice. In this article, we explore how you can separate fake news from the truth.

What Is Fake News?

There are two kinds of fake news:

1. Stories that aren't true. These are entirely invented stories designed to make people believe something false, to buy a certain product, or to visit a certain website.
2. Stories that have some truth, but aren't 100 percent accurate. For example, a journalist quotes only part of what a politician says, giving a false impression of their meaning. Again, this can be deliberate, to convince

"How to Spot Real and Fake News," Emerald Works Limited. Reprinted by permission.

readers of a certain viewpoint, or it can be the result of an innocent mistake. Either way, it quickly attracts an audience and can become entrenched as an "urban myth."

Note: To confuse matters further, there are also people who claim that factually accurate stories are fake news, just because they don't agree with them or find them uncomfortable.

Where Does Fake News Come From?

Fake news is nothing new. But, what is new is how easy it's become to share information—both true and false—on a massive scale.

Social media platforms allow almost anyone to publish their thoughts or share stories to the world. The trouble is, most people don't check the source of the material that they view online before they share it, which can lead to fake news spreading quickly or even "going viral."

At the same time, it's become harder to identify the original source of news stories, which can make it difficult to assess their accuracy.

This has led to a flood of fake news. In fact, one study found that more than 25 percent of Americans visited a fake news website in a six-week period during the 2016 U.S. presidential election.

But, not all fake news stories are found online. Co-workers who gossip by the water cooler or while browsing print publications that fail to check their facts, for example, are also guilty of spreading misinformation, even if inadvertently.

The Impact of Fake News in the Workplace

Research shows that 59 percent of people are concerned about the effect that fake news has in the workplace, and with good reason!

For example, some people might start to believe that they no longer need evidence to back up their arguments. Others start to mistrust information all together. They stop listening to industry reports, and disengage from official workplace communication, slowing their professional growth and development. Ultimately, this can damage an organization's learning culture.

Fake news can affect behavior, too. It encourages people to invent excuses, to dismiss others' ideas, to exaggerate the truth, and to spread rumors. This can create divided, anxious workplaces where people are cynical and unsure of who to trust.

They might even begin to mistrust you if they believe that authority figures have lied to them, or that the information that they are working with is suspect. This can sap people of the curiosity, enthusiasm and ambition that they need to collaborate and to be successful.

Misinformation and fake news can also harm your business. Invented reviews of your products or inaccurate financial updates, for example, can do serious reputational damage.

Six Ways to Spot Fake News

Separating fact from fiction accurately can seem daunting. But getting to the truth is always worth the effort—even if it's not what you want to hear! Use these six steps to weed out the truth from the lies:

1. Develop a Critical Mindset

One of the main reasons fake news is such a big issue is that it is often believable, so it's easy to get caught out. Much fake news is also written to create "shock value," that is, a strong instinctive reaction such as fear or anger.

This means it's essential that you keep your emotional response to such stories in check. Instead, approach what you see and hear rationally and critically.

Ask yourself, "Why has this story been written? Is it to persuade me of a certain viewpoint? Is it selling me a particular product? Or is it trying to get me to click through to another website? Am I being triggered?"

2. Check the Source

If you come across a story from a source that you've never heard of before, do some digging!

Check the web address for the page you're reading. Spelling errors in company names, or strange-sounding extensions like ".infonet" and ".offer," rather than ".com" or ".co.uk," may mean that the source is suspect.

Whether or not the author or publisher is familiar, stop to consider their reputation and professional experience. Are they known for their expertise on the matter? Or do they tend to exaggerate?

Be aware that people who spread fake news and "alternative facts" sometimes create web pages, newspaper mockups, or "doctored" images that look official, but aren't. So, if you see a suspicious post that looks like it's from the World Health Organization (WHO), for example, check the WHO's own site to verify that it's really there.

Remember, even if you got the story from your best friend, this gives it no extra authority—they likely didn't follow these steps themselves before forwarding!

Tip: Trusted online fact-checking sites like Snopes can help you to verify stories that sound too good to be true.

3. See Who Else Is Reporting the Story

Has anyone else picked up on the story? What do other sources say about it?

Avoid leaping to the conclusion that all main stream media (MSM) output is fake. This can be as unwise as following every rumor or conspiracy theory.

Professional global news agencies such as Reuters, CNN and the BBC have rigorous editorial guidelines and extensive networks of highly trained reporters, so are a good place to start. But no one is unbiased, and anyone can make a mistake, so keep looking.

4. Examine the Evidence

A credible news story will include plenty of facts—quotes from experts, survey data and official statistics, for example. Or detailed, consistent and corroborated eye-witness accounts from people on the scene. If these are missing, question it!

Does the evidence prove that something definitely happened? Or, have the facts been selected or "twisted" to back up a particular viewpoint?

5. Don't Take Images at Face Value

Modern editing software has made it easy for people to create fake images that look real. In fact, research shows that only half of us can tell when images are fake. However, there are some warning signs you can look out for. Strange shadows on the image, for example, or jagged edges around a figure.

Images can also be 100 percent accurate but used in the wrong context. For example, photos of litter covering a beach could be from a different beach or from 10 years ago, not the recent alleged event.

You can use tools such as Google Reverse Image Search to check where an image originated and whether it has been altered.

6. Check That It "Sounds Right"

Finally, use your common sense! Bear in mind that fake news is designed to "feed" your biases, hopes or fears.

For example, it's unlikely that your favorite designer brand is giving away a million free dresses to people who turn up to its stores. Equally, just because your colleague believes that two married co-workers are having an affair, doesn't mean it's true.

Tip: Some stories that you'll encounter will sound "wrong," but won't necessarily be fake news. They could be intentional satire or something that comes from a humorous website, like The Onion or The Daily Mash, for example.

Warning: If these tips suggest that the information that you are about to pass on is fake, partial or malicious, avoid sharing it with others—even if you're inviting them to check it. Doing so could lead to rumors spreading and may harm your professional credibility.

Journalism Needs to Practice Transparency in a Different Way to Rebuild Credibility

Michael Palanski and Andrea Hickerson

Michael Palanski is associate professor of management at Rochester Institute of Technology, where he teaches classes in leadership, organizational behavior, and business ethics. Andrea Hickerson is director of the School of Communication and associate professor of journalism at Rochester Institute of Technology. Her research focuses on journalism routines and political communication.

Public trust in media continues to hover near all-time lows, driven by perceptions that the news industry is partisan and peddles inaccurate information ("fake news"), as well as ambivalence about news from social media.

According to a new Knight Foundation report on news media trust, transparency is a key factor in restoring trust.

Although media organizations promote the inherent value of transparency, they often do not explain what it means in practice.

In contrast, research in business organizations points to a clearer meaning and more specific practices of transparency that, if applied to journalism, could help journalists regain greater public trust.

What Does Transparency Look Like Now?

There are many definitions of transparency in journalism.

The Society of Professional Journalists' Code of Ethics defines transparency as "explaining one's decisions to the public." The recent report from media funder the Knight Foundation referred to transparency in journalism as "disclosing potential conflicts

"Journalism Needs to Practice Transparency in a Different Way to Rebuild Credibility," by Michael Palanski and Andrea Hickerson, The Conversation, March 22, 2019. https://theconversation.com/journalism-needs-to-practice-transparency-in-a-different-way-to-rebuild-credibility-111474.

of interest and making additional reporting material available to readers."

Both of these definitions suggest that transparency should constitute some sort of explanation to the consumer about the decision-making involved in the story.

These could be in the form of editorial disclosures that would explain, for example, if there was reader backlash to a story, why an editor felt a story was newsworthy, like in the case of the *New York Times* profiling a white nationalist.

Or there could be a longer "story behind the story," published as a sidebar that explains both how and why a story was reported, such as Vice News did when covering ethnic cleansing in the Democratic Republic of Congo.

In practice, however, transparency in journalism is most often treated as a simple transaction between news organizations and their audience. Two common examples are journalists hyperlinking to original data sources that provide evidence for a story's claims or nonprofit journalism organizations listing their sponsors.

But research in organizational management shows that while both the explanation and disclosure aspects of transparency are important for building trust, they are not enough and they need to be coordinated. In fact, by practicing only a partial version of transparency, journalism may well be harming itself and further damaging the public's trust in its work.

Where Transparency Falls Short

Organizational scholars Andrew Schnackenberg and Edward Tomlinson have proposed that transparency in organizations actually consists of three parts: disclosure (information is released in a timely manner), accuracy (information is correct), and clarity (information is understandable in context by the intended audience).

To understand how this definition of transparency could help media organizations, consider a recent example where the media reported on a controversy without the benefit of all three elements.

Prompted by the revelation that a Virginia governor's 1984 yearbook page had a photo of a man in blackface on it, *USA Today* recently released a story about racism in college yearbooks.

Reporters reviewed over 900 yearbooks from 120 colleges and universities published over the past few decades for the story. The story that they wrote describes the pervasiveness of racist pictures in university yearbooks. (This article mentions a racist picture from our own university, Rochester Institute of Technology.)

USA Today also published a story behind the story, whose stated purpose was "to be as transparent as possible about what we found." The supplemental article described the process by which photos were identified and analyzed.

The supplemental story states: "We found questionable photos virtually everywhere we looked—what amounted to a montage of everyday, casual bigotry memorialized among pages that captured daily life on campuses. Many of the photos did not have captions, making it difficult in some cases to determine what was going on. It is possible that some were part of a school play or had other explanations. But we built our report around images that had little or no ambiguity."

This supplemental story seems to be an attempt at providing some clarity about the main story by helping the reader understand the motivation and process for writing the main story.

The supplemental story, however, does not provide full clarity. There are no images of the offending photographs in their larger context within the yearbooks, for example. Similarly, the supplemental story lacks disclosure; there is no comprehensive list of the 900 yearbooks or the 120 schools surveyed.

We believe that providing clarity (examples in context) and disclosure (a list of sources) would allow readers to independently verify the data in the story.

In this example, using Schanckenberg and Tomlinson's definition of transparency could have led to better journalism—to a story that readers could trust more fully.

Competence, Integrity, Benevolence

Drawing on earlier research about trust, Schnackenberg and Tomlinson suggest that greater transparency can improve trustworthiness in organizations by helping to improve the public's perception of their competence, integrity and benevolence. Those are the three key building blocks of trust.

What would this look like transferred from a traditional business to a news organization?

The news organization would report events in a way that is understandable and accurate and act according to its stated values, and its primary goal would be serving the public interest.

So when a news organization discloses—to the extent possible—its sources and own motivation for doing a story, it helps to build perceptions of integrity and benevolence. When it makes an effort to bring clarity and accuracy by explaining the overall context of a story, or when it provides insight into its own decision-making processes, it helps to build perceptions of competence and integrity.

How Not to Do Transparency

To understand how the more nuanced definition of transparency borrowed from organizational business research can help news organizations build trust, consider the cable news network CNN. It recently hired Sarah Isgur Flores, a spokesperson for former Attorney General Jeff Sessions, to lead its 2020 election coverage.

As the *New York Times* noted, Flores was hired as a "political editor, not a pundit, and departing an administration in which the president routinely criticizes the news media, including CNN."

CNN's own media reporter, Brian Stelter, wrote about the hiring and the associated outcry about a political hack being placed in charge of supposedly objective reporting. His reporting verified the initial report from Politico, and Stelter wrote about Flores' previous employment in his lead. It was an attempt to bring transparency to CNN's actions.

But CNN executives would not speak for attribution with Stelter to defend the hiring, instead preferring to provide anonymous responses.

So, while Stelter attempted to tell the "story behind the story," he was rebuffed by his own network.

This was confusing for audiences trying to understand Flores' hiring as a political editor.

If CNN had accepted a definition and practice of transparency that included accuracy, disclosure and clarity, perhaps they could have given better thought to how this hire would be perceived and how they might publicly comment on it.

In the end, Flores announced that she will be a political analyst instead of an editor—a change in title she, not CNN, initiated.

When an important concept like transparency is only partially applied, it leads to something of a transparency trap. Media organizations may believe they are acting transparently, but incomplete attempts at transparency may damage credibility and thus do more harm than good.

Reporting Is Out, Punditry Is In

Tobe Berkovitz

Tobe Berkovitz is a College of Communication associate professor of advertising. He worked for 30 years as a political media consultant and appears frequently on television and in the press as a political and media analyst.

Most readers of this piece are likely very satisfied with the current state of the media. They probably also are college-educated, have a job that lets them work remotely, and live in a neighborhood with a desirable zip code.

Many of the 70-plus million Americans who voted for soon-to-be-former President Donald Trump see the media through a different lens. Not all accept the Trumpian trope that the media is fake, but many are likely to believe the media holds them in contempt and fails to accurately reflect their lives.

According to a recent Gallup poll, 60 percent of the public have "not very much trust" or "no trust at all" in the media, 9 percent "trust the media a great deal," and 31 percent "trust the media a fair amount." In 2008, 43 percent of Americans "trusted the media a great deal or fair amount." The phenomenon of the public's perception of the media has been relatively consistent for over a decade. Did Trump taint this environment? Definitely yes, but the media had a head start in generating this problem.

Let's look under the hood and evaluate how we got to the current state of the media, which is such an important foundation of democracy.

Complaining about the media is a long tradition in American politics. George Washington bemoaned his treatment by the press. This was the era known as the partisan press since outlets were dominated by the political parties and served as attack dogs brutalizing politicians in the opposing party. President Andrew Jackson was the warm-up act for Trump, with support from the rural masses and constant brawling with the media. Even President Lincoln was not immune from strong criticism and felt under siege during his presidency and reelection campaign.

The modern era of presidential battles with the media was launched by President Richard Nixon and his entourage of hit men, including Pat Buchanan (a Nixon speechwriter and senior advisor) and Vice President Spiro Agnew. The press was termed "the nattering nabobs of negativity" by conservative columnist and Nixon speechwriter William Safire.

Donald Trump fired the afterburner of hatred and distrust of the media. Unlike his predecessors, his was a relentless 24/7 assault on the entire media ecosphere. Press conferences, White House scrums, appearances on conservative talk radio and cable news, and his ubiquitous use of Twitter drove the message of fake news. In true Trump fashion, he branded the approach for fighting the media.

In isolation, these tactics could be damaging, but because it reinforced preexisting perceptions of the media, and more importantly, disruptions occurring in the media industry, as well as popular culture, technology, and consumer behavior, the impact has been devastating.

There is truth in the phrase the consumer is king/queen. Consumers are their own editors and program executives, selecting content that fits their tastes, ideology, and political leaning. They vote with their mouse and clicker, selecting content they want when they want it. And they have countless options satisfying their partisan preferences. Rachel Maddow, Tucker Carlson, Anderson Cooper, Rush Limbaugh, and an endless smorgasbord of social media and digital choices. It's all on their mobile devices for constant access.

Trump will be out of the White House, but will he be out of sight and mind? Not a chance. He is, and always was, the ultimate self-promoter, the maestro of clickbait and ratings gold. Leslie Moonves [Hon.'06], while president of CBS, famously said of Trump, "It may not be good for America, but it's damn good for CBS."

Clay Travis writes on OutKick: "Now that he's lost, they've killed their golden goose laying golden eggs." Much of the media is in economic dire straits, and if it doesn't have Trump to "kick around anymore," ratings, readership, and finances will take a hit.

The media has a small festival of introspection after significant changes in the political environment, but will avoid analyzing core problems that caused the decline in public trust.

Leading this parade is how cable news has denigrated the definition of news content. Reporting is out. Punditry is in. Objectivity is out. Partisanship is in. The "panel of experts" has poisoned the well and contributed to the cratering of trust and respect for journalism in general. The battle of the talking heads raises tempers and shakes viewers by their collars, but does little to inform them of the issues affecting their lives.

Clever quips and rapier barbs replace serious discussion. Most of the pundits are former politicians and campaign operatives with an ax to grind and a convenient stage on which to grind it. Reporters invited onto the set sink to the level of clever banter established by the regulars and morph into witty practitioners of the winning sound bite.

The most serious problem facing the media is the domination of Facebook, Twitter, and Google for the consumption of news as well as defining what is news and prohibiting what it blocks as "misinformation and false news." Silicon Valley becomes the Ministry of Truth. Journalist A. J. Why wrote, "Freedom of the press is guaranteed only to those who own one." Now owning a printing press is a quaint concept compared to the power of the overlords of social and digital media.

Perhaps too many planets are aligning for the media to recover from the era of Trump. Perhaps too many problems existed before Trump took the escalator down the marble atrium of Trump Tower.

But perhaps the power of the American people will prevail and get the media they ideally deserve.

The News Has Become Opinionated Entertainment

Sharaf Rehman

Sharaf Rehman was professor of communication at the University of Texas Rio Grande Valley.

Political figures, consumer products, and social institutions do not become credible or trustworthy instantly. While love may happen, at first sight, relationships, friendships, and trust are cultivated gradually, over long periods. At the same time, political credibility and trust do not erode overnight. The pivotal role played by credibility in the process of persuasion was argued in the early writings of Aristotle and has been revisited continuously by scholars in social psychology, sociology, political science, philology, and communication.

For a social order to function, its people must trust its institutions. To develop this argument, this paper will first offer an operational definition of trust and its three key elements—the source, the message, and the medium. It will then proceed to discuss the functions and dysfunctions of the mass media. Using a survey (N=126), the final section explores the level of trust in the American news media among Hispanic-American college students. Not unlike much of the American population, the level of trust in the social institutions and the media is low among the surveyed sample.

What Is "Trust"?

Trust is different from faith or confidence as defined in the field of psychology and sociology. Faith requires no fact checking. It is accepted as untestable truth. Having confidence in a person or

"The U.S. News Media: Is it News or Opinionated Entertainment? An exploratory study," by Sharaf Rehman, *French Journal for Media Research*, https://frenchjournalformediaresearch.com/lodel-1.0/main/index.php?id=1459.

an institution requires some degree of reliability in past behaviors on which one may place one's confidence. These differ from trust, which requires conditionality and solidarity. To a certain degree, both faith and trust imply the impossibility of checking the intentions or character of the party. Confidence and trust rely on exchange systems; confidence requires "structurally determined situations" while trust is an "unconditional exchange" (Seligman, 1997, p. 171).

Nearly six decades ago, Carl Hovland and his associates at Yale advanced the theory that messages from credible sources produced stronger attitude changes and associated levels of trust corresponded to the "speaker's expertise and trustworthiness" (Hovland et al. 1953).

Social psychologist Coleman (1990, p. 98), argued that trust was based on rational choices and "interaction between trustor and trustee. If a trustee is trustworthy, the person who places trust is better off than if the trust was not placed, if the trustee is untrustworthy, the trustor is worse off than if the trust were not placed." Thus, trust in news media requires ethical and professional behavior from journalists (Fukuyama, 1995). Silverstone (1999) asserted that for economies and societies to function, it was necessary for people to trust other people.

Source Credibility

Although newspapers have editorial sections where the editors and columnists write opinion pieces, the audiences expect media sources (reporter, anchorperson) to remain fair and unbiased, accurate and trustworthy, and to tell the whole story covering diverse points of view. Under no circumstances should the reporters' own opinions surface as part of the coverage. Once reporters deviate from this strict demand, they come to be perceived as opinion pundits and cease to be impartial messengers.

Message Credibility

People's overwhelming disregard for advertising and political messages is a fair indicator of people's general mistrust in advertising messages and campaign slogans. Credibility encompasses both objective and subjective components of the believability of a source or a message. Credibility has two elements: trustworthiness and expertise. Both have objective and subjective dimensions. Once the credibility of a source becomes suspect, its messages become suspect. Finberg (2002) asserts that credibility is hard to earn and even harder to regain once lost. For example, it may be a while before consumers will accept advertising messages originating from VW auto group or Wells Fargo Bank. In a similar vein, people are cynical about the news media because the media are cynical about themselves (Capella & Jamieson, 1997). Mistrust in the media is compounded by elements such as media's failure to report and erroneous reporting (Major & Atwood, 1997). When such incidents occur, the media themselves cover such carelessness and mistakes, reducing people's trust in the media (Watts et al. 1999). The sole currency of a message is the integrity of its source, i.e., the reporter. The only currency that media have is their credibility. When one medium makes a mistake, it affects the credibility of the rest of the news media (Shepard, 2017).

Credibility of the Media

A medium (newspaper, radio, television, the Internet) is just that—a medium. It delivers a message. The credibility of a medium is tied to the credibility of the messages. As such, messages become a matter of credibility of a medium. Media credibility is an interaction of source, message, and receiver (Wathen & Burkell, 2002). During and immediately after World War I, newspapers were perceived as more credible than radio. It was in the early 1960s when television began to be viewed as more credible than other news media (Westley & Severin, 1964). Newhagen and Nass (1989) suggested that people considered newspapers as institutions and broadcasters as individuals, thus using different criteria when determining the credibility of print media (newspapers) vs. broadcast media (radio and television). Thus, the news from the newspapers was institution based, and news from radio or television was personality based. With increasing popularity of the Internet, scholars have focused their attention on the newest medium (and the social media) and found that the Internet is seen as more credible than traditional media (Johnson & Kaye, 1998). However, many users of the Internet are unaware that most information posted online does not go through the strict processes of fact-checking and verification characteristic of traditional media (Flanagin & Metzger, 2000), nor do people always rank the more credible media as their preferred source for news (Westley & Severin, 1964). As scandalous yellow journalism put the credibility of newspapers in jeopardy, television is in part responsible for the deterioration of U.S. social capital (Putnam, 1995). As Engel (2017) argues, the 2016 presidential election put the American media credibility into the spotlight. The most trusted news media in the U.S. are the BBC and *The Economist*. ABC News, with the biggest audience, has to preface its newscasts as "The News You Can Trust." Americans say they get most of their political news from local TV, Facebook, and major networks like CNN and Fox News (Engel, 2017).

The Decline of Trust in Media

To trust implies having confidence in the integrity of someone, something, or some institution. As such, a trustor expects honesty, fairness, and transparency from the trustee. There was a time when people could expect such behaviors from their leaders, financial institutions, manufactures, and the news media. However, leading to the 2016 presidential election in the U.S., Americans' trust in the media "to report the news fully, accurately, and fairly" declined to a record low since the beginning of Gallup's polling history. Only 32% of the polled said they had a great deal or fair amount of trust in the media. This was an 8% drop in one year (Swift, 2016).

Gallup began such surveys in 1972. Confidence and trust of Americans in their news media reached its peak in 1976 (72 percent) when the media offered investigative journalistic coverage of the Vietnam War and the Watergate mishap.

Two significant changes took place during the Reagan years. Firstly, reporters and journalists were no longer permitted entry to places where American troops were actively involved. The journalists and reporters were required to be briefed and vetted by the Pentagon before going to war zones and were only allowed in places deemed safe by commanding officers. All text and images were to be cleared by field officers before journalists could file their stories (Croteau & Hoynes, 1999).

Secondly, media ownership drastically changed. The Federal Radio Act of 1927, the formation of the Federal Communication Commission in 1934, and the TV Licensing Freeze in 1948 were originally created to guarantee public access to clear radio and TV signals, necessary for accessing basic news and information, and to create a marketplace that permitted easy entry and access without monopolistic controls by large corporations. However, ensuing deregulation of media industries by President Ronald Reagan allowed larger corporations to acquire unlimited number of newspapers, magazines, radio stations, and television stations in any geographical market in the U.S. The result was as expected—media oligopolies and virtual control of all news and information by large corporations operating with the mission that the bottom line is the top priority.

Traditionally, profits for radio and television networks came from entertainment programs and the news divisions lost money. The consolidation of media ownership resulted in severe cutbacks in news staff that affected news coverage and quality. Declining readership of newspapers, loss of the three major networks' viewers to cable, and the revenue losses coupled with the popularity of 24/7 news and social media have impacted the viability and sustainability of the conventional news operations. Even though most "trained" journalists, whether traditional or digital, practice the journalist's code of ethics by fact checking and source verification. However, terms such as "fake news" and "alternative facts" have cast a shadow of doubt over most of the news outlets. Paradoxically, deregulation harmed diversity, localism, and competition in media, and accelerated the decline in media credibility to the extent that the mass media are no longer viewed as a credible institution that was expected to perform certain functions in American society. The rise of social media and big data (Amazon, Facebook, Google) have allowed for greater transparency, but it has also affected media credibility (Anderson & Rainie, 2012). Li & Suh (2015) hold that both medium and message credibility are key ingredients in the perception of online information.

Functionalism

Functionalism, as a theoretical framework, emerged out of an interest to understand the effects of mass communication on social order. The movement began with political scientist Harold Lasswell (1948, p. 37), who proposed that the mass media had three important social functions. The first was surveillance of the environment by keeping an eye on the political system and the social institutions and playing the role of a watchdog; the second was correlation of parts of society, and building cohesion within the parts and segments of a society; the third was cultural transmission, i.e., information about the past events and previous generations.

To these three, Charles Wright added "entertainment" as a fourth function of the media (Wright, 1959). Merton (1949) added two dimensions to functionalism. He asserted that either media functions can be intended (manifest), or they may be unintended (latent). He also stated that while media serve important functions in a social system, if media were to fall into the wrong hands, the senders of the messages might also use it for dysfunctional purposes (Merton, 1949). For instance, instead of exposing corruption, the media may choose to look the other way and cease to function in their capacity as a surveillance mechanism. Through discriminatory and hateful messages, the media may divide the various minorities and subgroups instead of bringing them together, neglecting the correlation function. By distorting or omitting certain portions from historical events, the media may marginalize certain subgroups out of a national heritage. By offering excessive amounts of graphic violence and poking fun at certain individuals, groups, or ideologies, the entertainment function may have a narcotizing effect making audiences disregard important social issues in favor of mindless entertainment.

The rise of fake news and alternative facts are some of the recent examples of dysfunctional use (abuse) of the media. While certain individuals or organizations may benefit from propagating fake news and offering alternative truths, the results are misinformation, segregated populations, and fabricated histories. The news organizations shift from information to profitability has brought the media credibility to a level where the audiences have become skeptical about the fairness, accuracy, and trustworthiness in the media reporting (Hickey, 2003; Meyer, 2009). While the role of the mass media in a democracy was to bring its citizens the information they needed to make important decisions, people no longer feel that the media can be relied upon for such trustworthy information.

A Survey of Public Opinion in 2017

Between the years 1998 and 2000, the *Wall Street Journal* held a 42% credibility rating; however, in 2004, it was down to 23%. *USA Today* has historically stayed below 24% and was down to 18% in 2004. According to Pew Research Center, which began reporting on media credibility in 2004, the credibility ratings for three major television networks in the year 2003 were: ABC 30%, CBS 33%, and NBC 29%. By the year 2004, the credibility of all three networks dropped below 25%. From the year 2003 to 2004, Gallup also reported a 9% drop in Americans' confidence in the media's ability to report the news accurately (Gillespie, 2004).

According to a study by the American Press Institute, for the news consumer, what makes something trustworthy and valuable differs depending on the topic and source, i.e., people tend to use different criteria for evaluating the credibility of national news vs. sports or lifestyle news (American Press Institute, 2016). The same study also reported that Americans follow a wide range of news and information topics. When asked to select the two topics they follow most closely, the most popular choices are domestic issues (25 percent), national politics or government (22 percent), local news (13 percent), and foreign or international news (4 percent) (American Press Institute, 2016).

The Gallup survey uses a shotgun approach to measure the credibility of the mass media. It asks respondents how much trust and confidence they have in the mass media such as newspapers, TV, and radio in reporting the news fully, accurately, and fairly. The choices offered are a great deal, a fair amount, not very much, or none at all. The present study uses a similar format to determine the performance of the media in terms of fulfilling the key functions discussed earlier and the overall perception of the media by the respondents. The study also examines the differences in these perceptions based on gender.

A 34-item, self-administered, paper-and-pencil instrument was given to college students on a public university with nearly 95% Hispanic Americans in a mid-size, border city on the U.S.-Mexican border. The questionnaire included items about the respondents' confidence/trust in social institutions, the U.S. government, the news media, and the economy. It also included items pertaining to political engagement, and interest in international, national, and local news. The instrument used Likert-Scale items for all the items except one. The exception was an open-ended question that asked: In your opinion, what is the most serious problem that the U.S. is facing now.

Participation was voluntary and anonymous. The survey was conducted two weeks after President Donald J. Trump took office. One hundred and twenty-six respondents completed the questionnaire. The aim of the study was to gauge the respondents' interest in local, national, and international news, how they accessed the news, and what levels of credibility the media and other social institutions had with the respondents.

The Sample and Trends

The sample comes from a border town with heavy traffic between Mexico and the U.S. providing many employment opportunities with Border Patrol, Immigration, Customs, Homeland Security, the police force, legal services, and the various law enforcement agencies. The local university offers a four-year degree program in Legal Justice that prepares the students for the above professions. Almost every family in the city has one or more of its members working for one of these agencies.

The sample consisted of 69 (54.8%) females and 57 (45.2%) males. Among the sample, 102 participants (81%) were between 20 and 25 years of age, 9 participants (7%) were under 20 years of age, and the remaining 15 (12%) were above the age of 25. Regarding their political position, 18 (14.3%) of the participants classified themselves as conservative, 63 (50%) as moderate, and 45 (35.7%) as liberal. The sample included 12 foreign students who were not eligible to vote. Among the remaining 114 respondents, 81 (71%) voted in the presidential election, and 33 (29%) did not take part in voting. It is reasonable to state that the sample consisted of politically engaged individuals. As for their political party affiliation, 69 (54.8%) respondents were Democrats, 27 (21.4%) were Republicans, 15 (11.9%) were independent, and another 15 (11.9%) said they were affiliated with some other political party. The county in which the survey was conducted has traditionally favored the Democratic Party.

Sixty-one (48.4%) respondents felt that the U.S. economy would remain unchanged in the next five years; 32 (25.4%) felt that it was likely to worsen, 33 (26.2%) felt it was likely to improve. A large majority, 75 (60%) of the respondents either agreed or strongly agreed that the image of the U.S. was likely to improve in the eyes of the rest of world in the next four years while 51 (40 %) disagreed or strongly disagreed.

The respondents' level of trust in social institutions, the U.S. government, the economy, and the news media was assessed using a five-point Likert-Scale. The items were worded as:

Consider the statement: "I trust …." Which of the following may apply to you?

I trust … completely.

I trust … for the most part.

I'm not sure

I mistrust … for the most part.

I have no trust in ….

Over one-fourth (26.2%) of the respondents have no faith in their politicians or the U.S. economy; nearly 29% do not trust the government. 33.3% of the sample has no faith in the legal system, and over 47% of the participants claim to have no trust in the media. In the present survey, the news media fare as the least trusted among the social institutions.

Men and women differed in their opinions about their trust in the U.S. government and the U.S. news media. Both Chi-square and t-test calculations indicated that women trusted the U.S. government more than men. This was significant at .01. Similarly, Chi-square and t-test revealed that men have a higher level of trust in the media than women do. This too was significant at .01 level. However, there were no significant differences in trust in the legal system, the U.S. economy, and politicians.

[…]

Regarding media functions, respondents rated the media's performance on a scale of one-to-five. The respondents' perception that instead of functioning as a watchdog, or being a cohesive force to unite various sub-groups, or providing an accurate and unbiased picture of past generations and history, the media are focused on providing entertainment and opinionated news coverage. The low scores on Cultural Transmission and Cultural Correlation suggest that there may be more of distortion of historical facts as presented in the media and that the media might be responsible for dividing various subgroups rather than uniting them. In this regard, the media may have become dysfunctional.

Regarding their exposure to, and interest in, the news, three (2.4%) of the respondents said they did not have much interest in the news, 87 (69%) said they were the light users of the news media, and 36 (28.6%) reported being heavy users of the news. Concerning their interest in different types of hard news, it appears that the respondents reported as being more interested in the national news. One-fifth of the respondents were not interested in the international news, and nearly one-fourth reported as having no interest in the local news.

Americans rely on many different types of media for news about the topics they follow most closely. No one medium dominates (American Press Institute, 2016). With the popularity of social media and smartphones as a delivery tool, it is not surprising that the respondents rely more on the new medium instead of the conventional news media such as newspapers, news magazines, radio or television.

The respondents use smartphones most frequently to access the news and information. However, it is unclear if the respondents access the news feeds from the television networks or from some opinion blogs.

[...]

Respondents seem to think that network television, MSNBC, and PBS carry a liberal bias while Fox and CNN lean towards conservative views. Nearly one-fourth of the respondents have little or no faith in FOX news channel or national newspapers. Nearly one-third have no faith in news magazines. Slightly over 50% of the participants never read news magazines, and 31% do not read newspapers.

Among the reported sample, women were politically more engaged than men were. A greater portion of the women voted in the 2016 presidential elections than did men. (Chi-square =11.344; p-value 3.441. This is significant at < .01.)

Regarding their party affiliations, proportionately more women claim to be Democrats than men are. Conversely, more men claim to be Republicans than women are. (Chi-square = 20.908; p-value < 0.0001. This is significant at $p < .01$.)

Regarding their outlook on the image of the U.S. in the next four years, 24 (42%) men agreed, and 33 (58%) disagreed; 51 (74%) women agreed and 18 (26%) disagreed. The calculated Chi-square = 13.108, p-value: 0.000294. The difference is significant at $p < .01$. Women are more optimistic about the future image of the U.S. in the coming four years.

Small sample size disallowed any comparisons among the Republican and Democrats, or politically active and non-voters, light and heavy users of the media, or those who claim to be conservative vs. liberal in their opinions towards the credibility of the institutions and the media.

It is, however, evident that the respondents' trust and faith in the institutions and the media are at historically low levels. Not only are younger people accessing unchecked and unverified news on social media, they admit to being disinterested, uninformed, or only mildly informed.

Conclusion

In conclusion, it is reasonable to say that the Hispanic-American college students who are 25 years of age or younger rely on smartphones and social media to access the news and information. As such, they have abandoned traditional print, broadcast, and cable media. According to the present sample, the function fulfilled by the media is that of entertainment. Newsfeeds on the internet, social media, and blogs are unchecked variations of the facts (alternative facts and fake news), and news events coated with opinions of the likes of Bill O'Reilly, Rachel Maddow, and Rush Limbaugh offer opinionated entertainment. There appears to be a dire shortage of programs providing investigative reports on matters that would be considered serious, national or international issues, i.e., the hard news. Soft news topics such as noisy neighbors, road rage, and heroes of American gymnastics hardly classify as investigative news journalism. However, such is more readily and frequently available on the television networks. Even serious television news programs such as *60 Minutes* and *20/20* structure their stories as fictional narratives with doses of good guys, bad guys, and conflict. Serious issues are dramatized to look like exciting entertainment. News reporting is reduced to storytelling (Postman, 1985). Resultantly, contemporary news anchors have failed to attain the credibility once associated with journalists such as Edward R. Murrow, Eric Sevareid, Walter Cronkite, Dan Rather, Connie Chung, Peter Jennings, Barbara Walters, and Tom Brokaw.

When the audiences lose interest in the news, and the news media turn national issues into entertainment, it is an indication that a nation may have become indifferent to its past or future. George Santayana warned us against such indifference to history by saying that those who failed to learn from the mistakes of their predecessors were destined to repeat them. U.S. involvement in Afghanistan and Iraq is reminiscent of the Vietnam War. The recent failed coup in Turkey reminds one of the Bay of Pigs incident and American plans for staging a regime change.

The author is aware of the limitations of the study due to its small sample. Thus, the findings are not generalizable. However, the findings do concur with similar studies conducted by other researchers, the Pew Foundation, and the Gallup Corporation. There is a need for further studies in assessing the decline in the credibility of the media and the social impact of such a change. There is also a need for refinement of the instruments to measure credibility and trust.

Fighting Misinformation May Be an Uphill Battle

Dietram A. Scheufele and Nicole M. Krause

Dietram A. Scheufele is a German American social scientist and the Taylor-Bascom Chair in the Department of Life Sciences Communication at the University of Wisconsin–Madison. He is also a Distinguished Research Fellow at the University of Pennsylvania's Annenberg Public Policy Center. Nicole M. Krause is a member of the Department of Life Sciences Communication at the University of Wisconsin–Madison, where she is a doctoral student.

Concerns about public misinformation in the United States—ranging from politics to science—are growing. Here, we provide an overview of how and why citizens become (and sometimes remain) misinformed about science. Our discussion focuses specifically on misinformation among individual citizens. However, it is impossible to understand individual information processing and acceptance without taking into account social networks, information ecologies, and other macro-level variables that provide important social context. Specifically, we show how being misinformed is a function of a person's ability and motivation to spot falsehoods, but also of other group-level and societal factors that increase the chances of citizens to be exposed to correct(ive) information. We conclude by discussing a number of research areas—some of which echo themes of the 2017 National Academies of Sciences, Engineering, and Medicine's Communicating Science Effectively report—that will be particularly important for our future understanding of misinformation, specifically a systems approach to the problem of misinformation, the need for more systematic analyses of science communication in new media environments, and a (re)focusing on traditionally underserved audiences.

"Science Audiences, Misinformation, and Fake News," by Dietram A. Scheufele and Nicole M. Krause, National Academy of Sciences (PNAS). Reprinted by permission.

[...]

What Does It Mean for Citizens to Be Misinformed or Uninformed About Science?

First, it is important to note that "misinformation" can be broadly defined as information that is incorrect, possibly by accident. Comparatively, "disinformation" has sometimes been used to denote a specific type of misinformation that is intentionally false. However, the distinctions between these terms—as well as terms like "rumor" or "fake news"—have not always been clearly drawn in research pertaining to these topics. Similarly, there has been some conceptual debate surrounding what it means to be "misinformed," compared with "uninformed." Being misinformed is often conceptualized as believing in incorrect or counterfactual claims. However, the line between being misinformed or uninformed—that is, simply not knowing—has long been blurry in different literatures.

For example, early empirical observers of the modern US political system equated being misinformed to not being informed in the first place, or to making decisions based on factors other than the best available information. "After examining the detailed data on how individuals misperceive political reality or respond to irrelevant social influences," Berelson et al. wrote over 60 y ago, "one wonders how a democracy ever solves its political problems." Much of the empirical work since then has focused on providing citizens with competencies to absorb relevant facts to "overcome areas of ignorance or ... correct mistaken conceptions." Thus, being misinformed has sometimes been understood as both holding inaccurate views and being uninformed about scientific facts and processes.

However, others have argued that believing incorrect information about both scientific topics (e.g., childhood vaccination) and political topics (e.g., weapons of mass destruction in Iraq) can have unique causes and consequences, especially if the person is also politically active. Compared with people who are uninformed or those who are informed but inactive, individuals who are "active" and "misinformed" have "unite[d] their purported knowledge and their political actions, [so] they have little incentive to abandon old beliefs, accept new ones, abandon old allegiances, find a new group, and change their behavior." Consequently, strategies to encourage people in different epistemic states to be "active" and "informed" might differ.

Of course, citizens can be uninformed and misinformed all at once—for example, they may be uninformed about how scientific processes work while being misinformed about the facts of a specific scientific issue—and these factors may influence each other. In practice, then, it is difficult to cleanly separate the "misinformed" from the "uninformed." Our goal, therefore, is not to tease apart these epistemic states, but rather to review what is known about individual-level "unawareness," "misinformation," or both, to identify what may be missing from proposals to improve those encounters and to bring these discussions to bear on the specific field of science communication.

Lack of Understanding of Science

One problematic area is citizens' understanding of basic scientific facts and the scientific process more broadly.

Knowledge About Scientific Facts

The US Science & Engineering Indicators (SEI) surveys measure factual knowledge about science biannually as the average number of correct answers to a series of true-or-false and multiple-choice items. Although such batteries of closed-ended factual knowledge questions are imperfect representations of what citizens know about science more broadly, these trend data suggest that knowledge of scientific facts and terms has not decreased significantly in recent years. There are differences across respondents, however, with factual knowledge being "strongly related to individuals' level of formal schooling and the number of science and mathematics courses completed."

Epistemic Knowledge About Science

Notably, recalling isolated scientific facts might have a limited impact on citizens' ability to make meaningful policy choices about risks and benefits surrounding emerging technologies. Likely more important is what has been called "epistemic knowledge"—that is, levels of information or misinformation among nonexpert publics about the scientific process and how this process shapes the findings produced by science. This is slightly different from discussions of "epistemic beliefs" more broadly, which can be understood as "beliefs about the nature of knowledge and how one comes to know."

Survey data on Americans' (mis)understanding of the scientific process does not show meaningful changes over time (with some variations due to coding of open-ended data). In the most recent SEI survey, one in three Americans (36%) misunderstood the concept of probability; half of the population (49%) was unable to provide a correct description of a scientific experiment; and three in four (77%) were unable to describe the idea of a scientific study, indicating an inability among "[m]any members of the public … to differentiate a sound scientific study from a poorly conducted one and to understand the scientific process more broadly."

Public opinion surveys also suggest that significant proportions of the public are concerned about how low levels of epistemic knowledge can negatively influence their own or other Americans' understanding of science news. Although there is certainly some complexity (and irony) in measuring individuals' perceptions of misperceptions among their peers, it is nonetheless interesting to note that two in five Americans (44%) agree that it is "a big problem" that "[t]he public doesn't really know enough about science to understand findings in the news," with only 16% not considering it a problem. Similarly, 4 in 10 (40%) think that it is "a big problem" that "[t]here are so many findings that it's hard to distinguish between high and low quality studies," with only 18% not seeing it as a problem.

Holding Beliefs Inconsistent with the Best Available Science

In *Theaetetus* Plato described knowledge as "justified true belief." Philosophical critiques of this definition have focused on the fact that people's reasonable, justified perceptions of reality, driven by their own direct observations of the world around them, can be inconsistent with truth. This highlights the unique role that science plays in society for providing citizens with information that is justified beyond their own observations because it is based on reliable, systematic bodies of scientific knowledge. In fact, the low levels of factual and epistemic knowledge discussed earlier would be less disconcerting if large proportions of nonexpert audiences would routinely defer to scientific judgment and make policy choices that are consistent with evidence-based consensus within the scientific community. Unfortunately, data do not always support this expectation.

Inaccurate Views of Scientific Consensus and the Willful Rejection of Scientific Consensus

In a 2014 US survey, two-thirds of respondents (67%) thought that scientists did "not have a clear understanding about the health effects of GM crops," despite broad scientific consensus on the topic. Similarly, half of Americans (52%) thought scientists were "divided" in the belief that the universe was created in the Big Bang, and about a third each thought that scientists were divided on anthropogenic climate change (37%) and evolution (29%). Of course, these data do not make clear the cause of these inaccurate views, which, arguably, could stem from people being uninformed, intentionally misinformed, or a bit of both.

Furthermore, split-ballot survey experiments have shown that even when Americans do seem to possess accurate knowledge of scientific consensus (however large or small that number may be for a given issue) there is no guarantee that they will integrate that knowledge into their attitudes or policy preferences. In other words, these respondents know what the scientific community has established as fact, but they nonetheless refuse to "know" it. Some have therefore argued that rejection of scientifically accurate accounts of the Big Bang or evolution by nonexpert audiences indicates neither a lack of information about scientific consensus nor the presence of misinformation, but, rather, motivated information processing.

Conspiratorial Beliefs

Another potential problem is persistent belief in conspiracy theories, or theories in which explanations for events and phenomena offer "as a main causal factor a small group of persons (the conspirators) acting in secret for their own benefit, against the common good." Conspiratorial beliefs can thus involve not only a willful rejection of scientific consensus but also false attributions of intent to members of the scientific community, as well as the fabrication of relationships between actors. For this reason, conspiratorial beliefs are typically understood as distinct from simple ignorance or misperception about isolated facts. Many of us believe in facts that turn out to be wrong. For instance, 7 in 10 Americans falsely attribute the statement "I can see Russia from my house" to Sarah Palin instead of *Saturday Night Live*'s Tina Fey. Many individuals, however, would adjust their views about this fact when presented with information showing their initial beliefs to be wrong. However, individuals who endorse conspiracy theories often refuse to adjust their belief systems when they are confronted with new and better information contradicting their misunderstandings.

Importantly, there is evidence to suggest that additional, traditional education will not be enough to dispel belief in conspiracy theories. For example, conspiratorial beliefs and inaccurate beliefs about scientific issues such as vaccine safety and climate change have also been linked to certain "epistemic beliefs," or broader convictions about how people can and should come to know what is true. Specifically, people who "[put] more faith in their ability to use intuition to assess factual claims than in their conscious reasoning skills" are particularly likely to support conspiracy theories, whereas people who believe that empirical evidence is needed to validate truth claims exhibit the opposite tendency. This is true even when issues have become politicized, leading to the conclusion that belief in conspiracies is "[f]ar from being an aberrant expression of some political extreme or a product of gross misinformation [but rather] a widespread tendency across the entire ideological spectrum."

It might be argued that survey respondents who express belief in conspiracy theories do not actually believe the falsehoods, but rather that they endorse certain conspiratorial views as a means of expressing their political or ideological allegiances, or to engage in a sort of out-group "mudslinging" (e.g., by claiming that Barack Obama is not American). Recent research, however, supports the claim that individuals actually do hold the conspiratorial beliefs they assert and are not simply engaging in "expressive survey responding." Unfortunately, conspiratorial beliefs often persist because the falsehoods that help to sustain them are repeated and "boosted" by politicians, corporate actors, fringe media organizations, and others to mobilize political support from their base.

How Does Misinformation Take Root, and Why Does It Persist?

Thus far our discussion has outlined the various ways in which people can lack accurate beliefs about science. Based on this overview, factors known to be associated with these varying epistemic states and proposed solutions can be examined across three levels of analysis: individual, group, and sociostructural.

Individual-Level Roots of Misinformation

Recent attempts to combat widespread misinformation have primarily focused on citizens' ability to recognize misinformation or disinformation and to correct their own views accordingly. As a result, proposed solutions often focus on the supply side of news, ranging from increased access to fact-checking sites to changing algorithms to stem the flow of fake news through various online channels.

The (In)Ability to Recognize Misinformation

Implicitly, most approaches to algorithmic curation of facts assume that citizens are misinformed because they are unable to sift through and critically evaluate information in emerging (social) media environments. There is no doubt that low levels of media literacy among citizens are part of the problem.

News and media literacy has been broadly defined as "the ability to access, analyze, evaluate and create messages in a variety of forms." Arguably, it is the "evaluation" skill that poses the most relevant challenge for misinformation, as those with limited ability to evaluate "cannot distinguish dated, biased or exploitative sources." A recent assessment of American students' media literacy demonstrates that the vast majority of them struggle to (i) recognize the possible biases of politically charged tweets and (ii) distinguish between a news story and news-like advertisement. Moreover, as the Pew Research Center reports, one in four (23%) American adults admitted to sharing misinformation via social media.

These circumstances have led some to argue that "the ultimate check against the spread of rumor, pernicious falsehood, disinformation, and unverified reports masquerading as fact" is a "generation of astutely educated news consumers" who can also function as competent digital content producers, and who can "identify for themselves fact-and-evidence-based news and information." Interestingly, others have critiqued proposals to increase media literacy by noting that these efforts have the potential to backfire, as "some media literacy skills could be used to justify belief in misinformation [and that] elite discourse about 'fake news' may decrease the public's trust in the media and their ability to recognize actual news stories without facilitating the identification of fake news." Consequently, these researchers suggest pairing news media literacy education with "activities designed to spur discussion about political issues."

Indeed, recent events such as the 2016 presidential election have brought increasing public attention to the role of social media in structuring and presenting information in such a way that may limit an individual's ability to assess the quality and usefulness of information, and to distinguish between fact and fiction. In response to mounting criticism of this kind, Facebook and others have proposed a dizzying array of technical remedies intended to bolster users' ability to identify misinformation and, generally, to make it easier for their users to have more "positive" information encounters. Unfortunately, their hasty attempts to diffuse criticism have often backfired or have the potential to backfire, which they have sometimes admitted.

For example, Facebook recently announced that it will prioritize the display of content that has been shared by users' friends and family members, and that they will see "less public content, including news, video and posts from brands," in an effort to offer users more "meaningful connections," and to ensure that Facebook is a force for good. However, this latter solution may cause people to see "more content that reinforces their own ideologies," and, in countries where these specific technical changes were piloted, frustrated users have reported that the modifications actually promoted the spread of fake news.

As technology companies continue to grapple with changes to their algorithms and interfaces, third-party fact-checking groups such as PolitiFact.com and Factcheck.org have also emerged to boost people's abilities to debunk misinformation, and efforts are ongoing to offer reliable, automated "deception detection" for both text and images. Furthermore, Google is working on real-time "fact check snippets" that appear as individuals search for disputed information, and computer scientists are devising solutions to automatically detect and combat the influence of "bots" (robots), which have been shown to successfully spread fake news with real-world consequences in both politics and the stock market. Finally, there is some evidence that correcting misinformation via an algorithmically driven "related stories" function on social media platforms can reduce misperceptions of science-related information.

Technical innovations like the ones above have been rightfully advocated for as possible solutions to the spread of misinformation. However, one unfortunate and defining feature of the posttruth era is that "facts and objective evidence are trumped by existing beliefs and prejudices," such that "a notable segment of the American public now subscribes to a non-standard epistemology that does not meet conventional criteria of evidentiary support." If it is indeed the case that facts no longer matter as much as they normatively should to some Americans, then technical solutions that make facts more recognizable or more visible will need to be supplemented by strategies that pair individual ability-focused solutions with solutions that address individuals' (lack of) motivation to seek out, consume, and interpret information in ways that privilege accuracy over other possible goals, such as the protection of their preexisting beliefs.

[...]

Outlook

Above, we discussed what it means for citizens to be misinformed about science, and what the processes are that may exacerbate or alleviate some of the strains on our democratic system originating from misinformation. Before shifting to implications of this existing body of work for the field of empirical science communication research, it is important to briefly outline a few nonobvious and potentially understudied actors that might—intentionally or not—contribute to the ability of misinformation to take hold in public discourse.

Collateral Influences

Actors that might inadvertently contribute to misinformation spreading among nonexpert audiences include scientists themselves, universities and science journalists, and, finally, readers of science news. As we discuss below, research is just beginning to understand the different roles that each group can play in ensuring that the best available evidence is heard in public debates about science.

Scientists

Some scholars have argued that decreasing public and policy support for science, among other factors, has created new incentives for scientific organizations to use mass media and other public-facing channels to promote particular findings or areas of research. Media, in turn, rely on celebrity scientists as resources for newsworthy accounts of breakthrough science. This has engendered concerns that hype and overclaims in press releases and other scientific communication can lead to misperceptions among nonexpert audiences about the true potential of emerging areas of science, especially if science is unable to deliver on early claims of cures for diseases, for instance.

While there is limited empirical work on the effects of hype or overclaims on misperceptions about science being wrong or producing contradictory findings, survey data suggests that these kinds of concerns are not completely unfounded. In national surveys, one in four Americans (27%) think that it is a "big problem" and almost half of Americans (47%) think it is at least a "small problem" that "[s]cience researchers overstate the implications of their research." Only one in four (24%) see no problem. In other words, while levels of confidence in the scientific community remain high, science may run the risk of undermining its position in society in the long term if it does not navigate this area of public communication carefully and responsibly.

Media

While the scientific community continues to enjoy a great deal of trust, public confidence in the press has declined substantively over past decades. In surveys, only 1 in 10 Americans (8%) express a "great deal of confidence" in the press. Similarly, three in four Americans (73%) think that "[t]he biggest problem with news about scientific research findings is the way news reporters cover it." Without a doubt, these poll numbers do not adequately capture all nuances of public trust in science or journalism as institutions. Even as imperfect indicators, however, they do not bode well for media's ability to better inform various publics about science or to even counter misinformation among publics that are particularly critical of science.

Part of the problem is related to a well-documented decline in science journalism and "the trend among many media organizations to no longer use (full-time) science journalists." As a result, coverage of scientific issues has often become the responsibility of political reporters, business writers, and journalists in other nonscientific beats. Paired with an increasingly polarized political environment, this has also promoted what some have called "false balance." The term refers to reporting—often by nonscience journalists—that puts established scientific consensus around issues like genetically modified foods or climate change on equal footing with nonfactual claims by think tanks or interest groups for the sake of "showing both sides."

Ironically, legacy media might also inadvertently be promoting their own demise by repeatedly and increasingly raising the specter of "fake news," which myriad political actors have framed strategically as a disease of traditional media specifically to discredit them. Indeed, a search on Lexis Nexis for appearances of "fake news" in newspaper coverage in the United States and globally reveals a clear increase in the yearly frequency with which newspapers have uttered this specific phrase and have arguably made more familiar—and therefore more believable—its false connotations.

This is not particularly surprising. Media are in the business of reporting on political discourse, including potential accusations of bias in their own coverage. Recent research, however, also suggests that frequent discussion of elite discourse about fake news in news media may affect whether individuals trust news media. As a result, media may inadvertently undermine public trust in their own work by providing a forum for accusations of bias and fake news put forth by political elites.

[…]

Underserved Audiences

A last area with a dearth of systematic empirical work are mechanisms to reach audiences that are often underserved by traditional channels for science communication. Newspapers, science television, or even science museums, for instance, tend to reach more educated and higher-income audiences. Furthermore, from work dating back to the 1970s on widening knowledge gaps, we also know that citizens with higher socioeconomic status (levels of education and income) are able to learn more efficiently from new information than their peers. As a result, quality scientific information is not only more likely to reach more educated and higher-income audiences, but, when it does, the ability of citizens with higher socioeconomic status to process new information more efficiently can further widen existing gaps between the already information-rich and the information-poor.

Our inability to reach all segments of the population equally well with high-quality scientific information is particularly troubling, given that the need for antidotes to misinformation might be particularly pronounced among certain groups of the public. One indicator of this problem is the educational and income gaps related to seeing fake news as a problem in the first place. In a 2016 Pew survey after the US presidential election, almost three in four Americans (73%) with a household income over $75,000 thought that completely made-up news caused "a great deal" of confusion. Comparatively, fewer than three in five (58%) respondents with a household income of $30,000 shared that concern. However, socioeconomic gaps also emerge with respect to people's confidence in their own ability to spot fake news in the first place. A 2018 US survey commissioned by *The Economist* asked respondents about their ability to distinguish real and fake news; 83% of respondents with a family income of at least $100,000 felt "very confident" or "somewhat confident" that they could "tell real news from fake news." Among respondents with an income of less than $50,000, that number dropped to 63%.

Those self-assessments might be overly optimistic across all segments of the population. Nonetheless, gaps in perceptions of fake news as a problem and gaps in the ability to meaningfully access corrective information across groups with different socioeconomic status are troubling based on normative democratic standards. Indeed, they are especially worrisome as new technologies like CRISPR or artificial intelligence (AI) raise political and societal concerns that are of particular relevance to audiences who traditionally have been hard to reach for science communicators. For example, applications of AI for self-driving cars and other forms of automated services are raising concerns about changing labor markets that might disproportionately affect blue-collar workers. Similarly, expensive therapies based on new genome editing techniques raise questions of equitable access to treatments regardless of patients' income or social status. All of these concerns will require political debates based on the best available scientific evidence. Those debates will have less-than-ideal outcomes if groups who will be significantly affected by these technologies are systematically uninformed or misinformed. Harnessing the science of science communication to ensure that socioeconomic disparities do not impact access to the best available scientific information for policy choices will therefore be crucial for the responsible development of these emerging technologies and new technologies in the future.

Organizations to Contact

The editors have compiled the following list of organizations concerned with the issues debated in this book. The descriptions are derived from materials provided by the organizations. All have publications or information available for interested readers. This list was compiled on the date of publication of the present volume; the information provided here may change. Be aware that many organizations take several weeks or longer to respond to inquiries, so allow as much time as possible.

American Press Institute
4401 North Fairfax Drive, Suite 300
Arlington, VA 22203
(571) 366-1200
email: hello@pressinstitute.org
website: www.americanpressinstitute.org

The American Press Institute advances an innovative and sustainable news industry by helping publishers understand and engage audiences, grow revenue, improve public-service journalism, and succeed at organizational change. For democracies to thrive, people need accurate information about the problems of civil society and the debates over how to solve them. That requires an economically sustainable, independent, and free press that is vested in the values of verification and monitoring the powerful, and is dedicated to putting citizens first, ahead of political faction.

Fairness & Accuracy in Reporting (FAIR)
124 West 30th Street, Suite 201
New York, NY 10001
(212) 633-6700
email: jjackson@fair.org
website: www.fair.org

FAIR is a national progressive media watchdog group, challenging corporate media bias, spin, and misinformation. It works to invigorate the First Amendment by advocating for greater diversity in the press and by scrutinizing media practices that marginalize public interest, minority, and dissenting viewpoints. It exposes neglected news stories and defends working journalists when they are muzzled. As a progressive group, it believes that structural reform is ultimately needed to break up the dominant media conglomerates, establish independent public broadcasting, and promote strong nonprofit sources of information.

Federal Communications Commission
45 L Street NE
Washington, DC 20554
(888) 225-5322
email: MediaRelations@fcc.gov
website: www.fcc.gov

The Federal Communications Commission regulates interstate and international communications by radio, television, wire, satellite, and cable in all fifty states, the District of Columbia, and US territories. An independent US government agency overseen by Congress, the commission is the federal agency responsible for implementing and enforcing America's communications law and regulations.

Gallup
901 F Street NW
Washington, DC 20004
(202) 715-3030
website: www.gallup.com

This global analytics and advice firm helps leaders and organizations solve their most pressing problems. According to its mission, it knows more about the will of employees, customers, students, and citizens than anyone in the world, and knows what matters most to them at work and in life and how those priorities change over time. The company then uses that knowledge to create transformation.

International Federation of Journalists

Rue de la Loi 155, B-1040
Brussels, Belgium
email: ifj@ifj.org
website: www.ifj.org

The IFJ, the world's largest organization of journalists, represents 600,000 media professionals from 187 trade unions and associations in more than 140 countries. Established in 1926, the IFJ is the organization that speaks for journalists within the United Nations system and within the international trade union movement. First established as the Fédération Internationale des Journalistes (FIJ) in 1926 in Paris, it was relaunched as the International Organization of Journalists (IOJ) in 1946 but lost its Western members to the Cold War and re-emerged in its present form in 1952 in Brussels.

Knight Foundation

200 South Biscayne Boulevard, Suite 3300
Miami, FL 33131-2349
(305) 908-2600
email: media@kf.org
website: www.knightfoundation.org

The Knight Foundation supports democracy in America by fostering informed, engaged, and equitable communities. The foundation invests in journalism, arts and culture in community, research in areas of media and democracy, and in the success of cities and towns where John S. and James L. Knight once published newspapers.

News Media Alliance

4401 North Fairfax Drive, Suite 300
Arlington, VA 22203
(571) 366-1000
email: info@newsmediaalliance.org
website: www.newsmediaalliance.org

The News Media Alliance is a nonprofit organization headquartered in Washington, DC. The organization was founded in 1992 through a merger of seven associations serving the newspaper industry and was originally known as the Newspaper Association of America (NAA). Its work focuses on the key challenges and opportunities of today's news environment: freedom of the press, public policy and legal matters, advertising growth, new revenue streams, and audience development across all platforms. The News Media Alliance is dedicated to working with its members, as well as other partner organizations, to advance the industry through advocacy, critical research and resources, and events that connect and inspire.

Online News Association

1111 North Capitol Street NE, Second Floor
Washington, DC 20002
email: support@journalists.org
website: www.journalists.org

The Online News Association is the world's largest digital journalism association. Membership includes journalists, technologists, executives, students, educators, and other digital media professionals. ONA's mission is to inspire and support innovation and excellence in digital journalism.

Pew Research Center

1616 L Street NW, Suite 800
Washington, DC 20036
(202) 419-4300
email: info@pewresearch.org
website: www.pewresearch.org

Pew Research Center is a nonpartisan fact tank that informs the public about the issues, attitudes, and trends shaping the world. It conducts public opinion polling, demographic research, content analysis, and other data-driven social science research. It does not take policy positions. It generates a foundation of facts that enriches the public dialogue and supports sound decision-making. It is nonprofit, nonpartisan, and nonadvocacy. It values independence, objectivity, accuracy, rigor, humility, transparency, and innovation.

Poynter Institute

801 3rd Street South
St. Petersburg, FL 33701
(727) 821-9494
email: info@poynter.org
website: www.poynter.org

The Poynter Institute is a global leader in journalism. It is the world's leading instructor, innovator, convener, and resource for anyone who aspires to engage and inform citizens. Poynter champions freedom of expression, civil dialogue, and compelling journalism that helps citizens participate in healthy democracies. It prepares journalists worldwide to hold powerful people accountable and promotes honest information in the marketplace of ideas.

Reuters

3 Times Square
New York, NY 10036
(646) 540-3000
website: www.reuters.com

With unmatched coverage in over 16 languages and reaching billions of people worldwide every day, Reuters provides trusted intelligence that powers humans and machines to make smart decisions. Founded in 1851, it has remained true to the Trust Principles of independence, integrity, and freedom from bias, working relentlessly to bring news from the source and from every corner of the world.

Society of Professional Journalists

3909 North Meridian Street, Suite 200
Indianapolis, IN 46208
(317) 927-8000
email: amonteleone@hq.spj.org
website: www.spj.org

The Society of Professional Journalists is the nation's most broad-based journalism organization, dedicated to encouraging the free practice of journalism and stimulating high standards of ethical behavior. Founded in 1909 as Sigma Delta Chi, SPJ promotes the free flow of information vital to a well-informed citizenry through the daily work of its roughly 6,000 members, works to inspire and educate current and future journalists through professional development, and protects First Amendment guarantees of freedom of speech and press through its advocacy efforts.

Bibliography

Books

Daniela Dimitrova. *Global Journalism: Understanding World Media Systems*. Lanham, MD: Rowman & Littlefield Publishers, 2021.

Linda Elder and Richard Paul. *Fact Over Fake: A Critical Thinker's Guide to Media Bias and Political Propaganda*. Tomales, CA: Foundation for Critical Thinking, 2020.

Adam Grant. *Think Again: The Power of Knowing What You Don't Know*. New York, NY: Viking, 2021.

Renee Hobbs. *Media Literacy in Action: Questioning the Media*. Lanham, MD: Rowman & Littlefield Publishers, 2021.

Bill Kovach and Tom Rosensteil. *The Elements of Journalism: What Newspeople Should Know and the Public Should Expect* (Revised and Updated 4th Edition). New York, NY: Crown, 2021.

Paul Levinson. *Fake News: Understanding Media and Misinformation in the Digital Age*. Cambridge, MA: The MIT Press, 2020.

Russell Muirhead and Nancy L Rosenbaum. *A Lot of People Are Saying: The New Conspiracism and the Assault on Democracy*. Princeton, NJ: Princeton University Press, 2020.

Cailin O'Connor and James Owen Wetherall. *The Misinformation Age: How False Beliefs Spread*. New Haven, CT: Yale University Press, 2019.

James O'Keefe. *American Muckraker: Rethinking Journalism for the 21st Century*. Franklin, TN: Post Hill Press, 2022.

Philip Patterson, Lee Wilkins, and Chad Painter. *Media Ethics: Issues and Cases*. Lanham, MD: Rowman & Littlefield Publishers, 2018.

Victor Pickard. *Democracy Without Journalism? Confronting the Misinformation Society*. Oxford, UK: Oxford University Press, 2019.

Robert M. Smith. *Suppressed: Confessions of a Former New York Times Washington Correspondent*. Lanham, MD: Rowman & Littlefield Publishers, 2021.

Joseph E. Uscinski. *Conspiracy Theories and the People Who Believe Them*. Oxford, UK: Oxford University Press, 2018.

Nikki Usher. *News for the Rich, White, and Blue: How Place and Power Distort American Journalism*. New York, NY: Columbia University Press, 2021.

Andrea Wenzel. *Community-Centered Journalism: Engaging People, Exploring Solutions, and Building Trust*. Champaign, IL: University of Illinois Press, 2020.

Periodicals and Internet Sources

Megan Brenan, "Americans' Trust in Media Dips to Second Lowest on Record," Gallup, October 7, 2021. https://news.gallup.com/poll/355526/americans-trust-media-dips-second-lowest-record.aspx.

FutureLearn, "Understanding Media Bias: How Credible Are Your Sources?" July 16, 2021. https://www.futurelearn.com/info/blog/understanding-media-bias-how-credible-are-your-sources.

Zaria Gorvett, "How the News Changes the Way We Think and Behave," BBC, May 12, 2020. https://www.bbc.com/future/article/20200512-how-the-news-changes-the-way-we-think-and-behave.

Elizabeth Jensen, "Looking to the Future: Restoring Public Trust in the Media," NPR, May 15, 2017. https://www.npr.org/sections/publiceditor/2017/05/15/528158488/looking-to-the-future-restoring-public-trust-in-the-media.

Ted Johnson, "Americans' Trust in Media Falls to 36% with Big Gap Between Democrats & Republicans," Deadline, October 7, 2021. https://deadline.com/2021/10/news-media-trust-gallup-1234852211/.

Saman Malik and Sarah Peterson, "How U.S. Media Lost the Trust of the Public," CBC News, March 28, 2021. https://www.cbc.ca/news/world/media-distrust-big-news-1.5965622

Andy Meek, "Fewer Americans Than Ever Before Trust the Mainstream Media," *Forbes*, February 20, 2021. https://www.forbes.com/sites/andymeek/2021/02/20/fewer-americans-than-ever-before-trust-the-mainstream-media/?sh=627eff05282a.

Politico Magazine, "Is the Media Doomed?" Politico, January 21, 2022. https://www.politico.com/news/magazine/2022/01/21/media-journalism-future-527294

Michael Schudson, "The Fall, Rise, and Fall of Media Trust," *Columbia Journalism Review*, Winter 2019. https://www.cjr.org/special_report/the-fall-rise-and-fall-of-media-trust.php.

Christopher Seneca, "How to Break Out of Your Social Media Echo Chamber," *Wired*, September 17, 2020. https://www.wired.com/story/facebook-twitter-echo-chamber-confirmation-bias/

Anjana Susarla, Dam Hee Kim, and Ethan Zuckerman, "2021 Was the Year of Fake News and Misinformation on Social Media. It's Going to Get Worse," The Print, January 1, 2022. https://theprint.in/opinion/2021-was-the-year-of-fake-news-and-misinformation-on-social-media-its-going-to-get-worse/792585/.

Amy Watson, "Credibility of Major News Organizations in the U.S. 2017-2021," Statista, August 31, 2021. https://www.statista.com/statistics/239784/credibility-of-major-news-organizations-in-the-us/.

Index

U

V

W

Y